Discipline from Birth to Three

Discipline from Birth to Three

How Teen Parents Can Prevent and Deal with Discipline Problems with Babies and Toddlers

**Jeanne Warren Lindsay, MA, CFCS
and
Sally McCullough**

Morning Glory Press

Buena Park, California

Discipline from Birth to Three
is part of the five-book *Teens Parenting* series. Other titles are:

Your Pregnancy and Newborn Journey: A Guide for Pregnant Teens
Your Baby's First Year: A Guide for Teen Parents
The Challenge of Toddlers: Parenting Your Child from One to Three
Teen Dads: Rights, Responsibilities and Joys

Library of Congress Cataloging-in-Publication Data
Lindsay, Jeanne Warren.
    Discipline from birth to three : how teen parents can prevent
and deal with discipline problems with babies and toddlers / Jeanne
Warren Lindsay and Sally McCullough. -- Rev. ed.
        p.   cm. -- (Teens parenting)
    Includes bibliographical references (p. 199-204) and index.
    Summary: Describes for teenage parents how to discipline
young children using teaching strategies rather than punishment and
offers the advice and comments of young parents themselves.
    ISBN 1-885356-35-8 (Hardcover)--ISBN 1-885356-36-6 (Paper)
    1. Discipline of children--United States--Juvenile literature.
2. Teenage parents--United States--Juvenile literature. [1. Teenage
parents. 2. Parenting.] I. McCullough, Sally. II. Title. III. Series:
Lindsay, Jeanne Warren. Teens parenting.
    HQ770.4.L56   1998
    649'.64--dc21   98-27894
                                                                      CIP
                                                                       AC

MORNING GLORY PRESS, INC.
6595 San Haroldo Way   Buena Park, CA 90620-3748
714/828-1998   1-888/612-8254
Printed and bound in the United States of America

Contents

Preface

Most discipline books are written for the parents of preschoolers or older children and ignore babies and toddlers. If your baby is under three, methods for disciplining older children aren't very important yet. You may need help for guiding your baby's behavior now.

The discipline methods you use during the first three years will have a big influence on your child's future behavior. This is a period of rapid change and learning. As you guide that learning in a positive way, you are truly disciplining your child. That is what this book is about.

We have worked with hundreds of teenage parents who all wanted the best for their children. As we talked in the parenting classes and in the infant center, the question of discipline came up many times. Too often, "discipline" seemed to mean punishment. The young parents themselves had been punished for misdeeds for as long as they could remember. They knew no other way to handle their child. Most had never had a chance to learn self-control. Their parents had tried to control their lives by punishing them.

Discipline means to educate. You have a wonderful opportunity to educate your child, to help her learn to behave, without punishment. It begins with trust. By meeting your child's needs in a loving, caring way, you will teach her to trust both you and her environment.

If you help your toddler satisfy her curiosity and comfort her when she is frustrated, she will learn that she is loved and respected. She doesn't have to be naughty to get attention. This kind of education is the foundation for the self-discipline your child will need throughout her life.

For this book we interviewed many teenage mothers and fathers (and former teenage parents) who told us how they felt about discipline. Parents of toddlers described their frustrations as their child "got into everything." We also interviewed older parents who had faced the stresses of being teenagers and parents at the same time. Many had lived with extended families. They had learned to cope with the involvement of other family members in the discipline of their children. They provide valuable insight into what it is like to start the parenting journey as teenagers, the journey you have just begun.

As each young parent is quoted, s/he is identified by age, children, and children's ages. Names have been changed, but the quotes and the ages given are always real.

You will learn as much from the comments of these teenage parents as you will from us. That's the way it was in our parenting class, and we think you will agree.

Good luck and best wishes as you continue your parenting journey.

Jeanne Lindsay
Sally McCullough   August, 1998

Foreword

As an early childhood educator, I came to appreciate and become totally fascinated with child development — the progression, the predictability, and the dependability of knowing how the stages take place and watching that happen with many, many children over the years.

I moved into a hands-on child development program with high school students and four-year-olds. I assumed these students were going to share my sense of wonder with the phenomenon called child growth and development. I soon learned, however, that these issues were not high on my students' list of priorities.

Then came the glorious opportunity to work with teen parents. How wonderful — here were these young eager parents with their own children. Surely one of the first things they would want to know is "How does my baby grow?" That is indeed one of the issues. They must cope, in addition, with many other aspects of daily survival.

Relationships of all kinds seem to be the key when

you're dealing with what is important and relevant to young parents. *One* of those relationships is "How do I deal with my baby? How do I discipline my child?"

When you have the right tools and materials, such as Jeanne's and Sally's book on direct and concrete issues of discipline and development, you can use the "teachable moment." Now the child growth and development comes alive . . . *now* it makes sense because she needs it. She wants to know! We can honor their parenting. We can turn parent, a noun, into TO parent, an action verb.

Amid the familiarity, the struggle and chaos of it all, it can be easy to forget that parenting is a sacred journey. It is a journey on which nearly half a million teenagers embark annually in the United States. For that journey, they need guideposts.

Discipline from Birth to Three honors that journey by being readable, understandable, and realistic. Young parents learn here that it's okay to be human; it's okay to make mistakes, and that they, too, can certainly be "good" parents.

This valuable resource is written just for teenage parents. It provides the guide for making their parenting journey a good experience for themselves and their children. I highly recommend it.

Marge Eliason, Founder
Young Families Program
Billings, Montana

Acknowledgments

We are grateful to Jean Brunelli, Pat Alviso, and Pati Lindsay who made time to read and critique part or all of this revised edition, and to all those who read the earlier edition. Their comments were invaluable. We also appreciate the valuable contributions of Richard Tefank, Chief of Police, Buena Park, California, and Sr. Ines Tolles, Soledad Enrichment Action, Inc., Los Angeles.

Perhaps even more important is the input from teenage parents and former teenage parents, the young people we interviewed, and whose wisdom is scattered throughout the book. For the first edition, 67 young people were quoted. For this revised edition, 54 more were interviewed, and many of this group are quoted here. They include Alysson Hall, Amber Wolf, Carlos Smith, Brandi Hatch, Danielle Alston, Erika Madrid, Gabriel Garcia, Harmony Tortorice, Isabel Franco, Janelle Byers, Katrina Amaya, Melisa Romero, Monica Hernandez, Noemy Calderon, Racheal Malonay, Robin Gardner, Robin Stanley, Rosa Paez, Stacy

Maloney, Tiffany Torres, Carlos Garcia, and Tina Mondragon. We interviewed others who are quoted and acknowledged in the other *Teens Parenting* series of books. We also appreciate the many other teenage parents whose insightful quotes are retained from the earlier edition.

David Crawford, teacher in the Teen Parent Program, William Daylor High School, Sacramento, supplied most of the photographs. His models were his wonderful students. Cheryl Boeller, Carole Blum, and Bob Lindsay also provided photos.

Tim Rinker is the cover artist, and Steve Lindsay helped design the book. We appreciate the contributions of these talented people.

Carole Blum and Karen Blake again helped with the proof-reading and kept Morning Glory Press alive and well during book production time.

We're especially grateful to our ever-supportive spouses, Stuart McCullough and Bob Lindsay. We love them.

Jeanne Lindsay
Sally McCullough

Ev, Cher, and Tom,
Mike, Steve, Pati, Eric, and Erin
who gave us practice in discipline
and who continue to give us their love.

With his parents' help, he will learn self-discipline.

1

Discipline Is Important!

I got in a big old argument with my cousin the other day. He said that all little kids at one time or another need a spanking. He said, "What if he tries to stick his finger in the outlet or eats a plant? Just say 'No'?"

Well, I think that might work better. I'm going to try communication first.

Adriana, 16 - Danny, 3 months

At the store one day Donovan wanted candy and I told him he couldn't have any. He started throwing a tantrum.

I left the store. I picked him up and left, leaving my stuff in the basket. I couldn't even shop.

*After that, when I tell him to stop screaming, he'll
cry and yell a little, but then he stops.*

                                    Belia, 17 - Donovan, 2

Questions Parents Ask

"How do I get my child to do what I want him to do?"

"Why won't she listen and behave as she should?"

"Will he ever learn that when I say, 'No,' I really
mean it?"

"How do I teach her to do as she should?"

Discipline is the answer. Knowing how to help your
child, in a loving and caring way, do what he really needs
to do is one of the greatest challenges of parenting.

Discipline Involves Caring

What do you think of when you say "discipline"?
Punishment?

Discipline means to educate. It comes from the same
root as disciple, one who is taught. In this sense, your child
is your disciple. It's your job to guide and teach your child
to behave in ways that will help him cope with the world he
lives in.

Discipline is an extremely important part of your task as
a parent. Setting necessary limits means you care about her.
You are concerned with her behavior and her future
welfare. Discipline is an expression of love.

Through discipline you teach your child to:

• Live within our cultural values.

• Get along with other people and respect their rights.

• Learn new skills and perform expected tasks.

• Feel good about himself and succeed in achieving a
  satisfying lifestyle.

• Learn to be self-disciplined.

Through discipline you teach your child not to:

• Hurt others or herself.

• Damage or destroy the things around him.

You begin teaching your child these values during his first three years. With your guidance, he'll gradually learn to modify his behavior to meet your expectations. How you guide him to reach these goals will not only affect his future behavior, but your relationship with him as well.

If you take the time and have the patience to discipline effectively now, you're less likely to have big discipline problems as she grows older. If you understand your child's developmental stages and work with her to achieve the above goals, you're more likely to have the well-behaved and caring child you hope to have.

Setting unrealistic goals for behavior or trying to care for your curious toddler in a non-child-proofed environment is hard, and frustrating for you and your child. The child cannot explore and learn as she should. She may not even be safe. The environment is probably somewhat dangerous.

You can discipline your child more effectively in a child-safe place that has many interesting things to explore and to use for play. It's best if an interested older child or adult is nearby who will talk to your child, someone who will play with her from time to time and help her when she needs it.

When your child is treated in this way, she doesn't need to be fussy to get attention or assistance. The most important part of discipline is making it *easy* for children to behave correctly.

Planning Ahead Helps

What really bothers me is the store. I still haven't conquered that. I tell Shaun that if he's a good boy I'll

get him a toy. One time I just left. I had to drop
everything, and it upset him a lot. It upset me, too.

Angelica, 20 - Shaun, 3

Dropping everything and leaving was probably the best
approach Angelica could take to teaching Shaun not to act
up in the store.

Not all environments are ideal. Sometimes you and your
child must wait in a doctor's office or in long lines at the
supermarket. You may not be able to avoid visiting homes
with lots of fragile knick-knacks. For these times, you need
to do extra planning to help him behave well.

For instance, a shopping trip will be easier if you plan to
go to only one or two stores and stay only a short time in
each. Finding ways to involve your child as you look and
choose your purchases will help, too. This works better
than trying to bribe him to be good.

When you must be out with your child, you can bring
along a favorite toy and perhaps a snack in case he gets
hungry. But even then it may be difficult. He can't be
expected to sit quietly or stand patiently. His interest span
is short and his body needs to move.

Try to limit these experiences. If they occur, remember
he isn't trying to be bad — he simply must move.

Lately Antonio has been something else. Yesterday
at the welfare office they had a little drinking foun-
tain, and he kept running over there. I brought him
back at least six times. I'd grab his arm and say,
"Don't do that!" Five minutes later he does it again.

I try not to spank. It has to be something really bad
to spank because I don't think spanking is a good way
to discipline. It's no more effective than saying, "No,
we don't do that."

Becky, 18 - Antonio, 26 months

The drinking fountain is a great new toy to explore. Does it really make a difference if he turns the water on? Or is Becky disciplining Antonio because of what *other people* think?

If you have more than one small child, going to the store or the welfare office is truly a challenge. Is it possible to leave at least one of them with someone else?

She Wants to Please You

She's not two yet, and already she likes to please us. When I'm stern with her, and I'm pretty big, she listens. Whether or not she does what I say, she knows something is wrong.

Two thoughts on this — try not to overdo it because if you do, it loses its effect. The other thing is that for the most part we're real nice to her, and she likes us and she likes being with us. When I say something stern, it matters to her.

John, 21 - Mandi, 22 months

"Already he likes to please us."

Most of the time discipline is not a difficult task. Your child by nature wants to please you. Usually she will try to behave the way she thinks you expect her to behave.

Her natural curiosity and her drive to explore will cause problems at times. All children need some help to control or limit undesirable behavior, but a caring relationship built on love and trust makes it easier for your child to accept limits to behavior.

Setting Limits

Limits provide guidelines for behavior. Because these limits will also restrict her freedom to explore and learn, set as few as possible.

Think about why you're setting the limit.

- Will her actions actually cause injury to herself or others?
- Are the materials really too fragile to be handled?
- Do things that are off-limits belong to someone else who might be upset if she uses them?

Sometimes a parent will set a limit because she feels someone else thinks she should. That's a poor reason. Don't set the limit unless you really need it.

Once you've set a limit, you've made a commitment to maintain it. It must be like a wall. You can push on a sturdy wall forever, but it will not give. You want the same strength in the limits you set for your child.

Annabel, 17 when the first of her four children was born, explained:

They just don't listen. They continually test you. They continually test to see where their boundaries are. Once they learn where those boundaries are, they seem to level off and behave much of the time.

With Dad's help, he's checking everything out.

You have to be consistent. With my kids I wrote down our rules. We have only two or three when they're little, and a few more as they get older. I explain that these are the most important, and they really have to stick.

Examples of our rules:

1. You can't run from us. It's hard to tell them that, but if you continually tell them, "No, you can't run away from us," they'll get the idea. Then if there is no running away from Mom, there won't be running into busy traffic or in parking lots.

2. There is no jumping on the furniture.

3. There is no playing in the bathroom. There are too many dangerous things in the bathroom.

4. Also no yelling, and that's a mom and dad rule, too. We can't yell.

This works for us.

Annabel, 27 - Andrew, 10; Anthony, 7; Bianca, 5; James, 2

Consistent limits help your child understand how you expect him to behave. They define safe play areas to explore and the materials that may be handled, examined, used for play, or even eaten. They provide a sense of security because he knows what he can do. He knows that someone is watching and caring.

A child without limits may have many unpleasant experiences and even injuries. He may become fearful and feel unprotected from danger, or he may seem wild or out of control.

I usually have to say something to LaShan once or twice, but I say it in a way that shows I mean business. I try to follow through on everything I tell her so she knows I mean what I say when I say it.

I tell her to put her toys up, and she'll run outside. I take her by the hand and take her back to her room and tell her to pick up her toys.

LaToya, 20 - LaShan, 3

She Will Test Her Limits

Every child tests her limits. Gradually she will learn to accept limits if they're suited to her development and temperament, and if they are warmly and consistently maintained. Some limits, of course, must be modified as your child grows and develops.

Sometimes a parent is surprised to learn her child is cooperative at his daycare center while at home he's quite the opposite:

Last year I put Ricardo in daycare for a couple of hours, and he was fine when he was there. I'd hear, "Oh, he's such a good boy." When I went over for lunch at school, he was terrible. His teacher said as soon as I left he was good again.

*It's probably because I tell him I'm going to do this
and I'm going to do that, but I never do it. What I
need to do is be more consistent. I'm more consistent
with Raul, and maybe that's why he's easier.*

Evangelina, 18 - Ricardo, 31/2; Raul, 27 months

When limits change frequently, the child is encouraged
to test to see which limits are truly real and which ones will
give way. Since he lacks both experience and judgment, he
may actually feel insecure and uncertain about what he is
allowed to do. His behavior may cause him to appear to be
naughty and foolish.

In any society people need to accept limits to behavior.
People unwilling to do this push on the limits society sets
and often get into serious trouble. They test limits to discover which are real and which ones they can get around.

This is a big problem throughout life for some people.
You don't want your child to carry such a burden. It can be
a tremendous disadvantage and lead to serious trouble.

She will learn about limits through discipline. Note, the
word is discipline, not punishment. *Punishment should not
be a part of disciplining babies and toddlers.*

Each Child Is Unique

*Our problem was we had two easy-to-handle
children and two that were difficult. We had to learn
that all children are different and have their own
special qualities.*

Annabel

Each child is unique and different from all other children. This makes parenting a real challenge. No one has
ever reared a child exactly like yours.

If all children were alike, or even if most children were,
perhaps a brilliant plan for discipline could be written. But

since children aren't alike, you need to be the expert on your own child. No one else can be that expert.

Respect for your child and her needs is the best starting point for discipline. Your expectations need to be related to her particular level of social, intellectual, and physical development as well as her temperament. An appropriate expectation for one child may not be right for her friend.

Parents with more than one child usually become aware quickly of the differences among their children. Cara's second child was extremely active when he was an infant, and became more and more difficult as the months went by. She discovered a way to help him:

I've had lots of problems with my middle child. Then I finally found out that letting Paul know how much I love him when he's good makes him want to be good. I let him know when I'm disappointed, but I love and kiss him and do special things for him when he's being good. He's made a 100 percent turn-around since I changed.

Cara, 24 - Leroy, 8; Paul, 6; Nicole, 5

Different Children — Different Methods

Is she a quiet child who doesn't get into much trouble? If you raise your voice, does she burst into tears? Or is she a very active baby who at six months is crawling to the coffee table and knocking things over?

Some children are very active and may have many discipline problems. Others may be easy to control. Obviously, discipline methods must vary with the child.

Patrick is extremely active, and my husband tends to feel everything he does is bad. Patrick stands on the back of the couch, he dances on the table, stands on the barbeque, and jumps off the picnic table.

*He's into everything, and his dad is constantly
calling him a bad boy. I suggest that he say, "What
you're doing is not right, but you aren't a bad boy."
He's mischievous, much more so than the others.
My children have progressively gotten more active,
and I have to deal with each one individually.*

Angelina, 28 - Steve, 13; Elaine, 10; Mike, 8; Patrick, 2

Children should not be labeled good, bad, bright, or
stupid. They simply should not be labeled. Yet people
apply labels so quickly to little children, and the children
are likely to live up to those labels. Let your child be her/
himself. As Angelina said, label the behavior, not the child.

Your child will have a more satisfying life if you teach/
discipline him well. And you'll enjoy him much more if
you take the time and have the patience to discipline him
effectively. *It's one of your most important tasks as
a parent.*

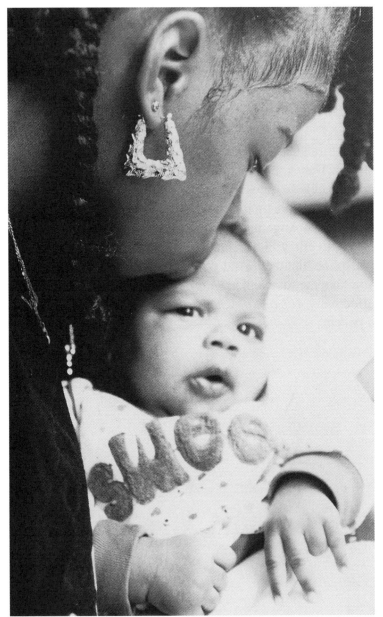

Disciplining your infant means
satisfying her needs as much as possible.

2

Infants
and Discipline

We always pick him up when he cries. Whitney kind of worries about spoiling him. She says she doesn't pick him up all the time because he's always going to be in people's arms. I suppose she could be right, but when I see him crying, I want to pick him up. So I do.

Randy, 17 - Keegan, 2 months

I can't let Shavone lie there and cry. I feel sorry, and I pick her up. Friends say, "Don't pick her up so fast. You'll spoil her," but I can't do that. In fact, I never let her cry.

Rene, 18 - Shavone, 1 month;
Vanessa, 19 months

Can You Spoil an Infant?

Discipline for your infant means meeting her needs in a gentle, loving way. Meeting her needs helps her develop trust in the people around her.

Trust is basic to her becoming a well-adjusted, caring human being. It is the foundation for self-discipline which is your eventual goal for her. Caring for your baby is a hard and exhausting task, but it's important to meet her needs as completely as possible.

Some people worry about spoiling a new baby. They caution that if you pick her up as soon as she cries you're only encouraging her to cry more often. But spoiling a new baby is impossible.

A hungry baby can't wait for food or comfort. When left alone in her misery, the baby only learns her world is not a safe place. She can't trust it to meet her needs. She is less likely to thrive in such a world.

When Sonia was a baby I'd try to guess what was wrong. I think babies have a reason when they cry. I'd be scared that something was choking her or that her head or her stomach hurt. I don't think babies cry just to be crying.

Estela, 18 - Sonia, 19 months

Estela is absolutely right — babies don't cry just to be crying. A tiny baby gets upset, even angry, if she doesn't get her food right away. Remember, hunger to your infant is a physically painful feeling.

Baby Is Self-Centered

The best discipline at this stage is for you to discipline yourself to meet your baby's needs as well as you possibly can. It's hard, though, for a parent always to be bright and sunny with a crying baby.

New babies are totally self-centered. They don't understand that you're exhausted or that you have too many things to do.

Of course there will be times when you'll be upset with your crying baby. Don't feel guilty about the way you feel. The important thing is how you actually respond to her.

Lacey cried a lot today. I tried as best I could to control myself. I did okay, but she knew I was upset because she was just staring at me. I felt real bad, and I began to cry. I love my beautiful girl.

Donna, 15 - Lacey, 3 weeks

As Donna discovered, your baby may react to your being upset by being more fussy. She senses your stress in your touch and the way you hold her.

Whether or not you sing well, your baby will love the sound of your voice. Perhaps singing to him will help relieve your tension as well as his:

What Vincent likes most is for me to sing to him while he's eating. I look into his eyes and talk or sing to him, and he opens his eyes wider and wider. Then he starts to close his eyes, and slowly goes to sleep. Sometimes he doesn't even need to eat. He just likes me to sing to him.

Alice Ann, 15 - Vincent, 3 weeks

Continue to Respond

For most mothers, the tendency to worry about spoiling comes a little later. When the baby is awake more during the day at about four months, for instance, you may be concerned. Perhaps those around you tell you you're already ruining him by going to him each time he cries.

Some babies may fuss a little when they're trying to

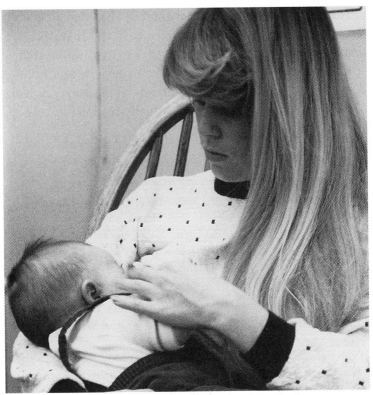

A hungry baby can't wait for food or comfort.

settle down, and may not need further attention. Crying, however, is different. It's important to continue to answer his cries and, in addition, play with him regularly. When you do, you'll probably find he takes less of your time and energy than he would if you let him cry. You'll feel much more satisfied, too.

In these first six months he isn't going to cry "just for attention" unless he needs that attention. Research data shows that babies whose cries are answered quickly cry less than babies who are left to cry until they stop. If you respond promptly to your baby's cries, he is actually less likely to become a spoiled, whining child.

Coping with Crying

For many babies, the two to six month stage is mostly a happy time. That doesn't mean she's always happy and easy to care for from the minute she's two months old until she's crawling. There will be difficult times with any baby.

When the kid is crying and you don't know what he's crying about, you start climbing the walls. I just remember that Nick is my baby. He didn't ask to be born. He is here because I wanted him. So I take care of him. I get upset sometimes when he cries and cries, but I don't show it to Nick. Sometimes my sister will hold him for five to ten minutes, and by that time I'll be all right.

Everybody gets those times. If you don't know what to do, and you can't handle it, you should give him to somebody else for at least five or ten minutes.

Theresa, 16 - Nick, 6 months

As Theresa said, everybody has those times. You, or someone close to you, may think you shouldn't feel like that. But these feelings are normal, and are okay. The trick is to keep the feelings from spilling over into unwanted action. Having someone else there to take the baby for awhile may help.

When I get really upset, I hold it in. I can't yell at Jay. He doesn't understand. He doesn't know right from wrong. I can't yell at him. It just makes him more upset. A lady down the street used to yell at her baby, and now that he's 5, you say something to him and he'll start crying. Sometimes I'll give Jay to Vince. He'll hold him for ten minutes while I go outside.

Bev, 17 - Jay, 8 months

Check to see if your baby is clean, dry, warm but not too warm, and doesn't seem hungry. If all these things are okay, but she still cries, hold her close. Rock her, walk with her. Some babies become calm when riding in the car. Others like soft music or even the sound of the vacuum cleaner. For other ideas for soothing a crying baby, see *Your Baby's First Year* by Lindsay.

When you're frustrated with her crying, remind yourself that she doesn't cry to be bad or to bother you. She cries because, for whatever reason, she isn't happy. You'll do what you can to make her feel better. At the same time, you, her parent, can't always make her feel good. You do the best you can.

Shaken Infant Syndrome

Sometimes a parent who would never spank her child may feel it's all right to shake an infant or child who is misbehaving. This is a physically dangerous thing to do.

An infant's neck is quite weak. At first he can't even hold up his head. The head of an infant or even a child is large and heavy compared to the rest of his body. If he is shaken, his head will bounce back and forth between his back and his chest. He's not yet able to stiffen his neck muscles to protect it.

At this young age, the brain is smaller than the skull. This allows room for the rapid growth of the brain. Therefore, as the head is shaken, the brain will be tossed around within the skull. The brain may become bruised and swollen. The shaking may cause some bleeding and blood clots as well. It can result in permanent brain damage or even death.

While many children will appear to survive a shaking without any handicap at all, they may not be as intelligent as they otherwise would have been. Problems with vision or learning may also appear later.

Even throwing a baby up in the air in play is not safe for these same reasons.

Keeping Bedtime Pleasant

If you satisfy baby's needs most of the time — feed her when she's hungry, pick her up when she cries, often visit with her when she's lonely — she'll probably go to bed with no great fuss most of the time.

Don't use bedtime as your most lively play period with baby. That won't help her accept being put to bed by herself.

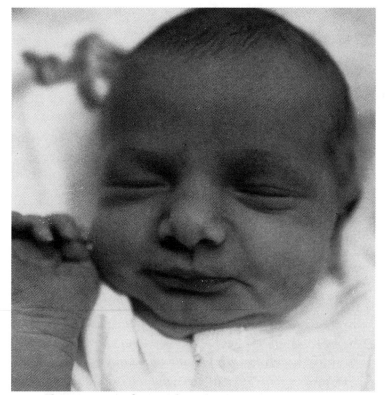

She may go to sleep without fussing most of the time.

This is a good time to start reading to her. At four or five months, she isn't going to listen to a long story, or even to a few Mother Goose rhymes. She probably will enjoy looking at some big clear pictures with you. Our favorite for this stage is a book with sturdy cardboard pages with a picture of a baby farm animal on each one. Our son, when he was a little older, insisted on saying "Night-night" to the baby pig every night for many weeks.

Sitting on your lap and looking at a few pictures now may help her feel ready for bed. It is also the first step in encouraging her to enjoy books.

I think Juan will learn a lot faster if I read to him. Right after I feed him before he goes to bed at night, I read to him. He likes the sound of my voice. I was reading "The Three Little Pigs," and I was using a gruff voice. He started to cry. Of course I changed to a softer voice.

Ginny, 17 - Juan, 4 months

Sleeping Through the Night

By the time he's two or three months old, your baby may sleep through the night, a real blessing for exhausted parents. He probably will still need a late night feeding. If you give it to him right before you go to bed, it may last him through the night. If he needs to eat again, try not to let the middle of the night become baby's playtime.

When they were babies, they slept in the same room with us. I nursed them, and usually by the time they were a month old, they would sleep through the night. If he woke up, I'd feed him and put him down.

I like to be organized, but with a baby you have to be flexible. You have to give yourself a little leeway. If he woke up in the middle of the night, I didn't make a

*big deal of it. I didn't change his diaper, but I would
feed him. I felt changing him would wake him up too
much. If the parent plays with the child when he
wakes up in the middle of the night, the baby thinks,
"Okay, you want to play."*
                              Annabel, 27 - Andrew, 10; Anthony, 7; Bianca, 5; James, 2

Annabel's advice is good. However, some babies would
need a diaper change at night in order to be comfortable.

Thumb Sucking Is Okay

Most babies suck their thumbs, some much more than
others. When she does, it's satisfying her need for more
sucking. Early thumb sucking will not harm her teeth. If
she's not nagged about it, she will probably quit when she
no longer needs the sucking.

*Juan sucks his thumb and was trying to suck his
hand. He couldn't get it in, so I gave him a pacifier.
My mom didn't want me to, but it was the only way I
could get him to sleep. I didn't want him to cry.*
                              Ginny

Can you imagine telling a baby not to crawl because if
she does, she may never want to walk? That's pretty silly.
But it's about as silly to tell a baby not to suck her thumb
because if she does, she may never want to stop. She'll stop
when she's ready.

Baby May Mirror Your Feelings

If a four-month-old baby isn't happy much of the time,
perhaps her mother and others around her aren't very
happy. Babies are great mimics. They are also extremely
sensitive little creatures and may mirror the attitudes of
their caregivers.

If Mother is unhappy, is she perhaps too tired? Does she have any help with baby? Can dad or grandma give her some assistance?

Is she perhaps feeling she is only giving, and not receiving much in return for her role as mother and, possibly, wife? Perhaps she's trying to keep up in school or perform a full-time job in addition to taking care of baby at home. No wonder she doesn't feel happy very often.

Louise tried hard to give her two children and her husband, Bob, everything they needed. She was trying to finish school, Meghan was only 17 months old when Mark was born, and Bob didn't help much.

I was quite upset with myself when Mark was first born. I didn't spend much time with him because of Meghan, and because I was trying to clean. Then I went back to school.

Mark was a demanding child. He wasn't very happy at first. I hardly ever saw a smile on his face until about three weeks ago. It worried me that no matter what I did with him, he was a crier.

I got upset, and so did Meghan. She would tell me the baby was crying. I'd tell her I knew. She couldn't understand why I would let him go, but I had tried everything. The only thing I could do was let him fuss and go to sleep, and he did sleep a lot. He apparently didn't feel very well during that time.

Louise, 19 - Mark, 5 months; Meghan, 22 months

Then several things changed. Louise graduated and was able to stay home with the two children. Mark started eating better. And then he giggled at his mother:

That brought me around. When he finally giggled, our world changed. Now he smiles most of the time.

Parent's Needs Are Important, Too

It's very important to your baby that mother and dad be satisfied with their lives. As a matter of fact, his parents' satisfaction is a big part of his own happiness.

If you feel frustrated, perhaps you need to get away by yourself occasionally. Share your feelings with a friend or relative. Find someone who is willing to babysit for a couple of hours. Many young mothers report a feeling of isolation and being "fenced in" with their baby care duties. Spending time with friends can help.

It is absolutely normal to want to get away from the kids sometimes. Don't feel guilty about it. We all need to be alone occasionally. I love my kids dearly, but sometimes I need space.

Thelma, 20 - Melissa, 4; Janeen, 18 months

You're Setting the Stage

During these first six months, you're setting the stage for your future relationship with your child. Disciplining yourself to meet her needs now will mean fewer discipline problems when she's older. Love her, play with her, help her feel comfortable. That's what discipline at this point is all about.

He'll be crawling soon.

3

He's Crawling — Help!

Dakota is eleven months old, and she's into everything. I grew up in a place where you couldn't spill juice. When she makes a mess, I feel like yelling, but we don't yell at her.

When I grew up, everybody was yelling, so that's what I do when I'm mad at Nathan (boyfriend). But he's quiet, and the more quiet he is, the louder I get.

We try not to argue in front of Dakota, but I'm sure she picks up on the tension.

Zandra, 16 - Dakota, 11 months

Nicklaus gets me mad, perhaps because I see a lot of me in

*him. I'm short-tempered, and when he starts to get me
mad, I get frustrated. Sometimes I don't know what
to do.*

*My mom and my sister are always telling me I
don't know how to raise my kid. And Nicklaus is so
stubborn —he wants stuff that's mine, like my neck-
lace and my keys. When he gets me mad, I find myself
yelling at him a lot. When he wants something, he'll
stop at nothing to get it.*

Theo, 19 - Nicklaus, 9 months

He Learns by Exploring

Discipline becomes a little more complicated during the
second half of the first year. Gradually your baby is becoming a person who needs a different kind of discipline than
she needed as an infant. Satisfying most of her needs for
food, warmth, cleanliness and companionship are no
longer enough.

She's learned many new skills, and she likes to practice
them. She throws toys, she bangs things together, and she
puts everything possible in her mouth. When she starts
crawling, she'll explore everything within her reach.

Now that he can creep or crawl, you may have a problem
if your home is not child-proofed. He wants and needs to
explore. That's how he learns.

Problem

*When Diego gets real fussy, sometimes he will
scratch me and pull my hair and slap me in the face. I
just pull his hands away and tell him "No." But the
more I tell him "No," the more he does it.*

Maudie, 17 - Diego, 11 months

One of the first things your baby may enjoy exploring is
your face and your hair. He may put his fingers in your

eyes. He will twist your hair around his fingers and may pull it. When he pulls your hair, he doesn't feel any pain, so he doesn't know it hurts.

If Maudie were to pull Diego's hair to show him how it feels, he would only be angry because she hurt him. Tying her hair back out of his way is a better solution.

During this second half of your baby's first year, you'll still need most of the discipline yourself. It is you who must stop the wrong behavior.

If he puts something dangerous or dirty in his mouth, it's up to you to take it out. Objects not to be touched must be out of his reach. You need to move him from unsafe areas, or you need to set up barriers.

Sometimes young parents (and older ones) find it hard to realize that babies at this stage don't understand what they should or should not do. They simply must explore because that's where they are in their development. They aren't spoiled, although Delia has a hard time agreeing:

> *Kelsey does bad things. He's demanding and he's spoiled. When he wants something, he wants it now. When I tell him "No," he doesn't seem to understand.*
>
> Delia, 16 - Kelsey, 7 months

Delia is right. Kelsey can't yet understand what his mother wants. Even if he could understand, a child Kelsey's age isn't able to wait patiently. While he must explore in order to learn, he doesn't understand the value or use of objects. Kelsey is not a "spoiled child." He is behaving normally for his age.

Slapping little hands that reach for things has little effect on correcting behavior. It can, however, threaten the trusting relationship you're building. It can also make future discipline more difficult.

Even though the responsibility to do something is mostly

yours, your patient guidance will help your child begin to
learn how she's expected to behave. Eventually she'll be
able to take more responsibility for her actions. Your
understanding and help during these early months is building a good foundation for self-discipline and self-esteem.

Play with Her Regularly

Spend time playing with her. Let her know you enjoy her
company. This provides good insurance against future
discipline problems.

She needs stacking and sorting toys now. As she plays
with them, she begins to understand the concepts of stacking, sorting by shape, etc. While it's a good idea to as-
semble her stacking and sorting toys and set them on low
shelves, it's a bit frustrating to have her brush them back
off the shelf almost immediately.

You may decide to keep a few of these toys out of reach.
Use them when the two of you play together. The rest
should be left out. You'll need to reassemble them frequently so she can learn from her play. She won't learn
much from a box full of pieces from various toys.

Constant Supervision Needed

When your baby is learning to stand, he'll want to
practice his new skill a lot. He will try to pull himself up by
hanging on to almost anything. A sturdy coffee table,
couch, or some chairs may be fine supports. He will also
try to pull himself up by grabbing the unsteady lamp or the
tablecloth.

You'll warn him of these dangers. Then he'll go right
back to try again. Someone will tell you he should be
punished. After all, he isn't "minding" you, he isn't
"listening."

He isn't trying to be irritating, but at this stage in his life, he doesn't understand your concern. He won't remember your warning. Besides, he simply can't control his strong impulse to grab whatever is available in his repeated attempts to stand.

If you can remove the tablecloth, do so. If the unsteady lamp can be banished from the living room for a few months, banish it. This is the best way to discipline at this age.

But maybe these are items that, for whatever reason, must stay. Then each time baby starts to pull on the tablecloth, you need to move him away at once. Show him a safe place to pull himself to standing. There should be many such places in your home. Tell him "No" as you take him away from the tablecloth.

Neither hitting, spanking, nor a raised voice is a good solution to this problem. Pulling to stand is a developmental need, something he must accomplish. If you spank him each time he goes toward that tablecloth, he may eventually tune you out. He may seem not to mind being spanked. Or he may become afraid. He doesn't know why you hit him.

Pulling to stand is a strong developmental need.

If you tell him, he won't understand.

Imagine how you'd feel: You're just learning the wonderful new skill of standing. In your eagerness to perfect this skill, you want to practice. But when you attempt to practice, your mother, the most important person in your world, hits you. That doesn't make sense.

Consistency is the key once again. If it's really important to you or to the people living with you, keep that tablecloth on the table. Your child will eventually mature enough to understand he must not pull on it. But he won't learn by being hit. His learning depends upon a lot of patient teaching from you.

For awhile you must be his control. You must set his limits and help him stay within those limits. Nagging and punishing a baby for forgetting your rules doesn't make sense.

He must first mature enough to understand and follow those rules. Each time he grabs the tablecloth, patiently take him away to an area where pulling to stand is safe.

Perhaps you're wondering, "Why so much concern about a tablecloth?" Most of us don't leave one hanging down where a toddler can pull it off the table.

True. But many families have other things around which are just as appealing. The important thing to realize is that the adults, not the child, must take the responsibility for dealing with these situations.

If you're unwilling or unable to child-proof your home, you must be willing and able to spend an enormous amount of time helping your child cope with his surroundings.

Meals Can Be a Hassle

Mealtime is torture for some parents of babies and toddlers. A baby can, and often does, disrupt a meal by demanding breastfeeding or a bottle just as the family is sitting down to dinner.

Before long, around six months, she's able to sit in the high chair. She probably wants to try to feed herself although it may seem she's only playing with her food. She probably finds food very interesting stuff to examine. She will pinch and squeeze it in her tight little fist, smear it on her tray like finger paint, or drop it on the floor while she watches it fall. Her spoon will probably follow.

Food is a new area of discovery, and she is busy exploring. Although it's rather unnerving for the other family members to watch, she's not trying to be naughty. She simply enjoys the feel of squished food.

You can, of course, limit this mess and still help her learn to eat. You could start by putting newspapers or a plastic trash bag under her high chair, especially if it's over a rug.

At first you'll do most of the actual feeding. At the same time, give her a spoon along with some mashed potatoes or other food that will stick to the spoon. Let her practice.

A small square of toast is nice for finger feeding. A small glass that she can get her hands around or a cup with a drinking spout will help prevent milk spills.

She still needs help while she's trying to figure out how to handle the spoon or the cup. If you put your hand over hers, you can help her guide it to her mouth. As her skills improve, her attention will gradually shift from food exploration to self-feeding.

If She Refuses Food

As she nears her first birthday, she presents a different problem. If she's eating table food, it seems even more reasonable to feed her while the family eats. This is a good social time for her, too.

But what happens when she's learned the power of saying "No," and refuses to eat? What if her mother is equally determined that she will eat? She may not bother to eat at all. Almost all toddlers play with their food to some extent, but some children seem to do little else. When he's about a year old, he may need less food. Soon, "No" becomes his key word. Mother may be worried that he isn't eating enough. If she coaxes her toddler to eat, his "No" will be more definite than ever. Besides, he probably gets a lot of attention for that "No." This reinforces his negative behavior.

Worrying about a toddler eating, watching him spit out his food, or seeing him dump his milk on the floor doesn't add much enjoyment to the family meal. But there are some positive things to do.

As mentioned earlier, place newspapers around his chair to limit the mess. Give him mostly finger food which he can handle himself. Most important, you needn't be all that worried about him starving to death or getting the right foods in his diet. He'll eat if he's hungry.

If you offer him only the foods he should eat, and you don't give him food containing lots of sugar or fat, he will probably eat a pretty balanced diet on the whole. He may eat carbohydrates one day, and protein-rich foods the next, but it will balance out. If you can be casual about his eating, mealtime isn't likely to turn into a discipline problem.

If you insist he eat when he doesn't want to, if you slap him for spilling his milk, or yell at him for playing with his food, mealtime will be miserable for everyone.

Some young mothers complain about grandparents giving their babies cookies and candy, perhaps even sips of soda. Grandma may think this is a sign of love.

If this happens at your house, perhaps you could suggest

a hug instead of a sweet snack. Then you can take responsibility for having nutritious snacks available. At this age, your child still needs snacks, but of course you won't give her junk food or carbonated drinks.

Not Much Memory Yet

Wendy isn't old enough to understand anything I tell her.

If I tell her "No," she doesn't know what I mean. If she's doing something I don't want, I take it away from her and give her something else.

Pati, 21 - Wendy, 10 months; Rosalind, 5

Does baby have a memory yet? Not very much. You can "test" her memory yourself.

Memory Test

Sit with her on the floor. Let her play with a toy for a few minutes. Then pick it up and put it under a scarf. Does she reach for it or look for it? If she doesn't, you know she simply doesn't remember the toy. It's gone as far as she's concerned.

Make a game of it. Put the toy partly under a blanket. Say "Find your toy." Does baby reach for it? She may not at first. Later, as her memory develops, you'll be able to cover it entirely and she'll remember to look for it.

Until your child's memory is well-developed, you can't expect her to remember that yesterday you told her to stay away from the coffee table. Memory develops gradually. Your patience during this stage is an important part of your long-term discipline.

Her short memory at this stage also makes it possible to substitute a toy or other plaything for the forbidden object she grabs.

Bedtime Routine

Do you have friends who have problems getting their child to go to bed and to sleep? You probably would like to make bedtime a different kind of experience for your child.

The habit of holding him while you give him his bottle is especially helpful as he begins to resist going to bed. At six months, baby will usually go to sleep if he needs to. By about nine months, however, this is not always so. By this age, baby is interested in so many things that he may not want to take time for sleep. You can help matters by setting up a nightly routine for him:

I have a routine. Ever since seven months she's started going to bed at a regular time, and by 8 she's asleep. We play a little while, then give her a bath. We take her into the kitchen for a drink, and we look at a picture book. Then we tuck her in. It works.

Stacy, 16 - Tiffany, 9 months

Reading to your baby at bedtime can calm him down so he'll be able to fall asleep a little easier. Rocking him to sleep is a method used by many parents.

If we don't rock Sonja before we put her to bed, she'll scream for an hour —but we can rock her to sleep in about 15 minutes. I don't mind, except I don't want her to be two years old and I still have to rock her to sleep. I want to be able to lay her down and she'll go to sleep.

Julie, 16 - Sonja, 7 months

Probably the majority of toddlers aren't willing to have mother simply "lay her down and she'll go to sleep," however. Most older children like to follow a routine and to be tucked in at night. Your baby will continue to need some special attention at this time.

Sometimes a change in beds or rooms will disrupt even a small baby's sleep schedule:

Jonita was sleeping really good through the night. Then I changed bedrooms with my sister and put her in a new crib. The past two weeks she's been getting up at night, and I usually give her a bottle. Sometimes she'll go to bed at 9 p.m., then get up at 11. If I'm still up, I let her play herself to sleep.

Ellen, 17 - Jonita, 6 months

Jonita may not really be hungry when she wakes up. It would probably be better for Ellen to try other methods of soothing her before resorting to an extra bottle. She might go in to Jonita, reassure her that she is there, perhaps pat her back for a few minutes. Jonita might go back to sleep at that point. If not, the next step might be to offer her a drink of water. Check her diaper. If she's wet, she probably should be changed.

Letting her stay up to play when she wakes up may be a habit Ellen would rather Jonita didn't acquire. Letting her stay up "if I'm still up" will cause real problems next week if Ellen is tired and wants to go to bed at an earlier time.

Keeping a Positive Attitude

Keeping a positive attitude toward your baby most of the time throughout his first year is possible if you remember his stage of development. He's not a "bad baby" if he can't control his urge to stand. He's not bad if he continually messes with things on your coffee table. At this point, you're his conscience.

The magic word, as we've said before, is supervision. While self-control is your ultimate goal for your child, it's *your* self-control that matters now.

Parenting is a big job, but your child is worth the effort!

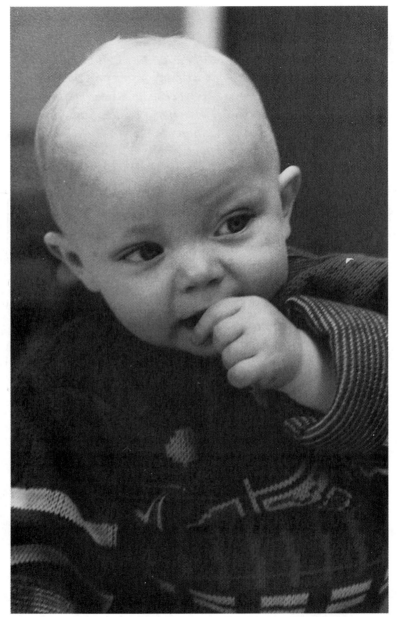

He needs to be able to satisfy his curiosity.

4

Child-Proofing
as Discipline

I put things out of Dakota's reach. I clean the room, make sure there's nothing dangerous for her to get into. Other rooms are more likely to be dangerous because of the other children, so we have to watch her constantly.

I just spend time with her. People tend to distance themselves by watching TV, and don't pay attention to the kids. Usually we try not to have the TV on much. It helps a lot if we spend time with Dakota.

Nathan, 20 - Dakota, 11 months

I don't want to kill Mandi's curiosity because that's what

*makes her want to learn. If you're always punishing
her for getting into a cupboard, she's going to learn
she's bad for investigating things.*

*When we child-proofed the kitchen cupboards, we
left four for her to get into. It took her a couple of
days to figure out which she could open.*

John, 21 - Mandi, 22 months

Helping Her Learn

If your child's curiosity is spoiled by too many "No"s
and other kinds of restrictions, she won't learn as well as
she should. Bluntly, she won't be as smart as she could be.

On the other hand, if she can satisfy her curiosity most
of the time, and if she has many different kinds of experiences and a variety of things to explore, she's getting a
good foundation for future learning.

For instance, she's learning about objects: that some are
heavy while others are light; some are smooth, others are
rough; some feel cold and others are warm; that metal feels
different from wood; that rugs feel different from bare
floors. The list goes on and on.

Her inner drive tells her that she must interact with her
environment in every way that she can: reaching out,
crawling, grabbing objects, banging them together,
throwing them, mouthing and tasting them, etc.

She is rapidly learning an enormous amount about her
world. The knowledge she gains provides a foundation for
all future learning.

*If it's something she just can't do, I'm going to put
it out of her reach. You can't expect a baby to understand not to do something she wants to do. If she's
taking a hammer to the wall, you take the hammer
away rather than just saying "No."*

John

She's learning about people, too. Hopefully she has discovered the comforts of being nurtured by people who love and care about her. Now she's learning how her drive to learn, her curiosity, is regarded by these most important people. If her eagerness to learn is valued and encouraged, she will experience even more fun and excitement in learning. She'll learn even faster. This child will undoubtedly want to learn when she goes to school.

You encourage learning when you provide a safe learning environment for your child. Many discipline problems will disappear at the same time. An environment of constant "No"s defeats the joy of learning and is a continuous challenge to good discipline.

Child-proofing your house or apartment is a key issue. You need to make your home safe for her. You also need to protect some things from your child.

Baby's Curiosity — Mother's/Dad's Anxiety

Shelly goes through the house finding everything. But it's always somebody telling her, "No, you can't touch that."

Dixie, 18 - Shelly, 17 months

Is nurturing his curiosity easy to do? Let's look at a typical living room complete with a couch, coffee table, lamps, chairs, television, and bookcase.

The floor lamp has an unsteady base and can be tipped over quite easily. One of the chairs is a fragile rocker mother doesn't want damaged because it was her grandmother's chair. On the coffee table is a glass bowl, a bouquet of artificial flowers, and several china figurines. Three family pictures framed and covered with glass are on the television. Against the wall is a little table. A pitcher and six glasses are setting on top of it. Books in the bookcase

He's very curious about everything. That's how he learns.

are not meant for children.

Now picture a ten-month-old baby in that room.

He has been crawling for several weeks. He is now learning how to pull himself to a standing position.

Next time someone tells you, "Oh, they have to learn. If he's old enough to touch it, he's old enough to understand that he must leave it alone," think of this room. The flowers, the bowl, the pictures, the figurines, the glasses, all are inviting. He is eager to explore, and at last his motor skills have developed to a point where he can begin. All of these items are waiting for his discovery.

But what happens? "No, you can't touch that."

"I told you, leave those pictures alone."

"Get away from those glasses."

"Put that bowl down this minute."

"Don't you dare touch those flowers."

Unfortunately, some hand slapping often goes along with all those orders.

Put yourself in his place. Do you still want to learn as badly as you did? Or does the situation remind you just a little of the strange state our schools would be in if teacher said, "Now this is what you're expected to learn today, but don't you dare open that book. You could tear the pages."

What if the science teacher said sternly, "Stay away from those microscopes. You'll get them dirty"?

Or did you ever hear of a music teacher saying, "Don't touch that clarinet. It might break"?

Maybe you want to leave the stuff out so you can teach the kids, but after it's too late, it doesn't do any good. Of course we teach them not to get into light plugs, some of the cupboards, etc.

But just to put knick-knacks where he can get them, then tell him he can't have them, is cruel. It's like putting a hungry person in front of a table of delicious food, then telling him he can't eat. Naturally a kid is curious — he wants to see and touch the pretty things.

Erin, 22 - Kelton, 7; Wayne, 9 months

Has someone suggested to you that the best way for a baby to learn the value of property is to leave things out where he can touch them? Then, they may add, you should punish the baby for handling those objects.

Most children punished in this way will eventually learn to leave those objects alone. They will also learn it's dangerous to explore. They may decide good books are to be avoided. They will realize that parents can hurt you, and that force is an effective way to control people.

We're going to keep stuff off the tables so we won't have to say "No" all the time. Janeen's mom has a

coffee table with little coasters, flowers, stuff like that.
We're talking to her about moving all that stuff away
from the living room and the kitchen. She's willing.

Jason, 18 - Josh, 3 months

Gradually, of course, your child must learn that some
things are his and some are not. Some things can be played
with and others can't. Before he's a year old, however, he
really can't cope with deciding just what he can explore
and what he can't.

First, his memory only recently started to develop. How
could he possibly remember today that you told him
yesterday to leave the flowers alone?

During his second year, he'll be a little more capable of
following your directions.

"How will he learn what 'No' means if I never tell him
'No'?" you may ask. Never telling him "No" is not likely to
happen. Can you imagine a home where a crawler or a
toddler doesn't have to hear "No"?

There will be many times when you must say "No."
You'll stop him from burning himself on the stove. You
won't let him stand up in his high chair because you don't
want him to fall. There are dozens of other things he'll have
to learn even if you child-proof your home as completely
as possible.

If he's told "No" all day long, no wonder he doesn't pay
much attention. But if, when mother says "No," she re-
moves baby from the forbidden activity immediately, he
will understand so much better that "No" means that
activity is not allowed.

Playpen Prevents Exploring

Do you plan to put your child in a playpen? Penning her
up for more than a brief period is guaranteed either to bore

her or infuriate her. Boredom is also a killer of curiosity, of learning. She doesn't learn much when she's angry, either.

I don't like playpens. I'd feel like I was caging Shelly in, just as if I were putting a leash on her. My mother always told me to get a playpen. She said I would regret it if I didn't, and that she would be into everything.

Shelly knows more because she hasn't been shut up like that. I know she would have learned things later if she'd been in a playpen. When she was getting into things, my mother would throw it in my face, but I don't think Shelly needed it.

Dixie

Many people believe a child in a playpen is wasting her time. She is separated from the things that interest her and spark her curiosity. She can't explore and develop

A child in a playpen can't satisfy her curiosity.

concepts. She is unable to practice most of her developing skills. There is no place to crawl or walk.

A child in a playpen is learning nothing about discipline. Supposedly she is in a safe place where she needs little attention. She probably gets next to none. She is like a toy put away in its place.

On rare occasions a playpen may be necessary. When you go on picnics or to the beach, you may decide to take the playpen along if your child isn't ready to play on the ground or in the sand.

Occasionally you must be involved in an activity that keeps you from observing your child, and no one else will watch her. You may need to use a playpen for a short period of time to keep her safe.

Many times you can work around such problems by finding a safe place for her to play. Keep her close to where you must be so you can watch her.

An older child may sometimes want to get in the playpen as an escape from the baby. He may appreciate a place to play with tiny things that must be kept away from a baby who still puts everything in her mouth.

Child-Proofing Your Home

When Brandt gets into something, I tell him "No" and pull him away from it. Then he sees something else to play with.

He likes to take all the jars out of the cabinets. We put the child-proof lock under the sink.

Sheleen, 15 - Brandt, 1

If you choose not to use a playpen, or to reserve it for short periods of time, how can you cope with your terrifically curious, still clumsy, whirlwind of a child? After all, your sanity and the sanity of other family members is also important!

We child-proofed our apartment. This has almost
totally eliminated problems because almost anything
Troy can get into is okay. If you eliminate the cause,
you don't have the problem.

When we go to someone else's house, he's pretty
good. I usually bring along a couple of toys, or point
out things he can play with rather than saying "No."

We had a playpen, but I didn't keep him in it much.
The doctor said, "You're dumb. It won't hurt him
to be in there two or three hours a day, and it will
give you a chance to get things done." But Troy
learned to entertain himself, and I could work without
him being penned up.

Rebecca, 20 - Troy, 21/2 years

Child-proof your home! Take a weekend if necessary.
Start out by crawling through the house at your child's eye
level. What does he see? What will look inviting to him?

You're looking for two kinds of things. First, you want
to remove things that would hurt him. Second, you want to
remove the things you don't want your child to damage.

If you like breakable decorative objects, find a high
shelf, preferably one close to the ceiling, for them. If you
must leave ash trays out, choose unbreakable ones. Then
take the responsibility of never leaving ash-filled trays
where your child can reach them because the cigarette butts
are poisonous. Expect the smokers at your house, not the
baby, to figure out a way to cope with this rule.

You'll also want to do all you can to keep your home
smoke-free. Babies and toddlers exposed to second-hand
smoke get more colds and ear infections. If someone in
your family smokes, will s/he at least go outside to smoke?
Your baby would be grateful.

You can get special locks for your kitchen cabinets
which will keep your child from opening the doors. Check

with your local hardware store.

Check your electric cords to make sure they're in good condition. Exposed wires are not good any time. They are especially dangerous when handled by a curious baby who puts everything he touches into his mouth.

Cover all unused electrical outlets with special plastic covers. Electrical outlets in use are very dangerous as well. Get all cords out of the way as much as possible. A baby is tempted to yank on the cord. Should he pull the cord only part way out and then put his fingers on the prongs, he would get a terrible shock. Figure out a way to put barriers in front of electrical outlets that are being used. Perhaps you can put a couch in front of one, a big heavy chair shielding another, etc.

Your bathroom and kitchen are safer for your child if your outlets are protected with Ground Fault Interrupters (GFI). These are required in new home construction, but older homes may not have them. These are available at home improvement stores, and they're not very expensive. They come with lots of directions. However, if you've never worked with electricity, you should get help in installing them. If you live in a rented place, talk to your building manager about installing GFIs.

Get rid of any extra house plants. If you can, figure a way to hang the ones you cherish from hooks in the ceiling, well out of your child's reach. Many house plants are poisonous. You can call your local poison control center for more information.

Even if the plant is not poisonous, pulling a heavy plant off a table onto himself could hurt your child. Besides, most plants aren't likely to survive the curious inspection of your toddler.

I'm putting things up. Lynn knocked over a plant
the other day and broke it. She was trying to stand up

by hanging onto the table, and she pulled it over.

Sheryl Ann, 17 - Lynn, 7 months

Some young couples box up most of their wedding gifts and store them for months, maybe years. They don't have space for their china and extra appliances in their tiny apartments.

Perhaps you can do the same thing as you baby-proof your house or apartment. Box up the bric-a-brac, the breakable dishes that aren't stored securely in cabinets, the artificial flower arrangements, the irreplaceable books. It will be fun to open these boxes later. In the meantime, you know your treasures are safe.

Help from Older Children

If you have an older child, or if you live with young brothers and sisters, child-proofing may be hard for them to

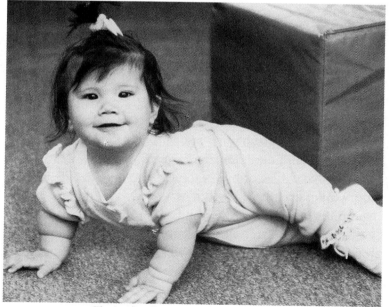

She's checking out the living room.

understand. They will be upset if your toddler damages
their things.

Some of their toys may not be safe for your child. Try to
help the older child understand how s/he will benefit from
keeping unsafe and/or cherished possessions away from the
toddler in the house.

> *The kids would come to me and say, "Cassandra
> scribbled in my book."*
>
> *I'd say, "She's a little kid. She's learning. It will
> help us all if there's not much stuff she can damage."*
>
> *So they started keeping their books in their room.
> Sometimes they'd even climb in the playpen to play
> with their little things. I told them they couldn't have
> tiny pieces all over because Cassandra would
> swallow them.*
>
> Kris, 17 - Cassandra, 25 months

Leave Safe Items Out

As you're putting away the things you don't want your
baby to handle, be alert for things she really couldn't hurt.

If she can touch, handle, and explore the item without
upsetting you or the rest of your family, and without danger
to herself, leave it out. She needs to explore. If you child-
proof to the point of having your living room and kitchen
empty, she can't do much exploring.

If you have a lot of bookshelves, you may decide to
empty them up to a three-foot height. Or you may realize
that books won't hurt your child and leave them on the
shelf. If so, make sure the books on those lower shelves
aren't especially valuable or hard to replace. She may tear a
few as she examines them. If you can handle that, leave
them in place.

Leave at least one bookshelf for baby's own books.

Perhaps another can store magazines she may look at without being scolded. However, she should not play with magazines if she puts the pages in her mouth. The print may not be safe for her to eat.

> *There is nothing on the bottom shelves of our bookcases. All the cupboards are child-proofed with baby locks on them. There is one bookcase in the den where we left all the books on the bottom.*
> *Todd can't get into the cupboards in the kitchen, and that aggravates him, but he gets a lot of freedom.*
> Jill, 18 - Todd, 16 months

This principle of giving him a drawer or shelf of his own applies to other areas in the house. If you have at least one kitchen cupboard he may explore to his heart's content, it's okay to put child-proof fasteners on the others.

Let him play in the cupboards containing pans and sturdy plastic ware. Cans of food also make delightful toys. In fact, he'll probably prefer your "toys" to his own.

> *I let Alice run through the house. I put a rubber band on the one cupboard I don't want her in. The rest of the lower cupboards she can explore all she wants. I shut each door in the long hallway.*
> Melanie, 15 - Alice, 13 months

If Grandparents Disapprove

> *When Kaylie started crawling it was hard. My mom wouldn't put anything up and I had to get the stuff and hold it to keep it away from her. I believe 100 percent in child-proofing, putting everything up high, but this isn't my house. She'd go for the same thing over and over. Finally she got over it, and now she doesn't grab things.*
> Samantha, 16 - Kaylie, 20 months

What do you do if you aren't in your own home? If you're living with your parents, they may not want to baby-proof their house or apartment. After all, they did all that when you were little, and that was enough!

You can probably understand their feelings. Maybe they're finally able to decorate their home as they want it now that you and perhaps their other kids are grown. It can be hard going back to the toddler stage, especially since they're "only" the grandparents.

Sometimes people forget how curious and carefree crawlers and toddlers are. Or perhaps you were a quiet baby who didn't get into things very much. Your child may be extremely active, and may be constantly investigating everything possible. You may feel that child-proofing as much as you can is the only way to go, but your parents think he should "learn" by being told "No." If it's their house, this can be a real problem for everyone.

> *Everything in my house is put away now. It was harder with Rosalind because we were with my parents. My dad smoked a lot, and he'd put things on the table without thinking. If Rosalind got into it, it was my fault, never his. You can't talk to my dad. He does not listen.*
>
> Pati, 21 - Rosalind, 5; Wendy, 10 months

Compromise Is Needed

Even young parents who realize the benefits of living with their parents for awhile often have mixed feelings about the situation. During the toddler stage, when baby is into everything, feelings may get especially tense. Glorianne's parents didn't think it was necessary to child-proof their house, for example. Danny was an extra lively toddler, however, and Glorianne disagreed:

Child-proofing is important at the one-year-old stage. You have to teach them not to touch some things, but there is no point in having endless temptations for them to get into trouble.

It took awhile to get my parents to agree, but finally I got some of the things put away. We made sure Danny was never in the living room so nothing in there was ever touched. In the den my mom put some things up. A lot of times when we were in there to-gether playing I would put more things out of his reach until we were done. Then I'd put them back.

He could explore within his limits, and that didn't frustrate anybody else. And he did learn not to touch.

Glorianne, 19 - Danny, 4

Glorianne illustrates the value of compromise. Because she was willing to keep Danny out of the living room, her parents were willing to have part of their home child-proofed for awhile.

Your parents may feel strongly that your child "has to learn" not to touch forbidden things. He can get hurt, however, while he's learning, and your parents don't want that to happen. If it's a glass object on the coffee table, he could get cut if he breaks it, or he could push it off onto the floor where it might land on his foot.

Leaving cleaning supplies where your child can get to them is dangerous because many of these materials are poisonous. A small child examines an object not only through sight and touch, but also by putting it in his mouth.

See *Baby's First Year* for more suggestions on making your home safe for baby.

Communication May Help

Ideally, you'll start talking about this situation long before your child is old enough to need a child-proofed house. If your seven-month-old crawler has just broken your mother's favorite antique vase, it isn't the best time to deal with the child-proofing problem!

If your family is firm about not wanting to disrupt their living area with child-proofing, perhaps you can arrange your bedroom to be as attractive and challenging as possible for your child. Fix things so she won't have to hear "No" constantly when she's in that room. You'll need to spend a lot of time there with her, of course, but this can work pretty well for the first year.

In the meantime, do all you can to be responsible about rearing your child. Don't leave diapers or baby things all over the house. Wash out baby bottles and clean up after feeding baby.

If you're careful about keeping this kind of mess cleaned up, your family may decide it's okay to rearrange the house for baby after all.

That's what my dad said at first, "Todd is going to learn." But Dad is the one who ended up putting more things away. I started putting things up, but he left some books out. He kept saying, "No, no," but finally he put his books away like the rest of us.

Jill

No Child-Proofing Means More Supervision

If your family doesn't see it this way, continue to allow your toddler as much freedom to explore as you can. Also plan to spend a large amount of time supervising, far more than you'd have to spend if you could child-proof.

You'll have to teach him slowly and patiently that he can play with this, but he must not touch that, over and over again. At times you may be able to distract him by substituting a toy for the forbidden object. Many times that won't work, and you'll need to comfort him as you move him away from the forbidden activity and try to help him understand.

Some children seem to adapt easily to such restrictions, others will not. Eventually he will mature and be able to accept these limits.

If you must raise your child in an environment with many restrictions, try to find places where you can take him to play more freely. If you don't have a fenced-in yard, is there a park nearby? Giving him a chance to run and play without constant "Stop that," "Quit running," "Don't touch that" comments will help him develop his curiosity and help you feel good about your role as a parent.

Kyle, who doesn't live with his son but sees him often, commented:

I take him to the park to play and we have a good time. Several of my friends have babies, and we go to the park together and have fun with our kids.

Kyle, 17 - Jonathan, 18 months

As you enforce the limits you must set for your child and, just as important, you continue to play with her and enjoy her, you'll be helping her grow into the self-disciplined person you want her to be.

Creating a good learning environment for her is a big part of your task.

Oozy mud is irresistible. This is how she learns about her world.

5

One to Two Years — Into Everything

Elena has always been a good baby, but she has her moments. Lately she's going through the Terrible Two stage where she wants to do only what she wants to do.

Now she tells us "No." I try not to yell at her, and I don't want to hit her.

She'll go after something on the furniture, and we tell her not to get it. We tell her "No," and she looks at us, then takes it. We take it from her, and she'll take it again, then throw the stuff.

Raul, 19 - Elena, 23 months

He loves pressing the buttons on the stereo, but
he's okay with us saying "No." Or I hold my hands
out to him, and he runs to me to be held.
You just have to keep trying to find what works.
                              Kaylene, 18 - Jayme, 16 months

He May Have No Fear

MacKenzie has been walking since he was nine
months old. People say it's easier when they get a
little older, but it's not. Now he's walking, he's into
everything. He threw our cordless phone in the toilet.
He unravels all the toilet paper . . .
                              Grechelle, 16 - MacKenzie, 11 months

When a child becomes a toddler, her discipline needs
change. Now she's able to walk. Her new independence
provides more opportunity to learn about her environment.
She can easily move from one place to another if it seems
more interesting.

She can grab objects that used to be out of her reach. By
climbing, she'll find even more to examine.

She's learning many important things. The child-
proofing you did earlier helps keep her explorations safe.
She can still get herself into serious trouble, however, if no
one is watching. She should never be left alone.

Manuel has gotten into stuff and ruined tapes so I
just have to keep everything up. He has a temper.
He's starting to throw fits. When you take something
away or tell him "No," he's real sensitive.

Discipline for him at this point includes the gate so
he can't get into the kitchen and play with the gas
stove. We keep his bedroom open, and he plays there
and in the living room. I don't let him into our room.
                              Kambria, 19 - Leesha, 5; Manuel, 14 months

Toddlers can easily hurt themselves. Some are fearless climbers. You may find him sitting on the dinner table trying to climb the bookcase, leaping off the sofa, or performing some other hair-raising activity. Yet, at one year of age he has little concept of the meaning of the word "No."

Memory Is Still Short

If we tell Robin "No," he runs (crawls) and laughs. If he's crawling up the stairway and we say "No," he crawls faster because he knows we're after him.

The reason I know he doesn't understand is, first of all, he's my third child. If you don't expect somebody to understand something that's good for him, how can he understand "No"? He knows if I call his name, but he's not going to understand if I say, "Don't do that."

Jennifer, 23 - Jarrod, 5; Jason, 2; Robin, 1

Through the use of gestures, your year-old child is able to tell you quite a few things. Now she has some words, too. She's learning to talk. It's easier to understand her wants and to talk to her.

She may even follow simple directions. But don't expect her to "mind" you or follow your commands long after you have given them. She simply won't remember.

Directions given from a distance are useless. Some days in her effort to explore, a toddler will appear to go from one thing she shouldn't touch to something else just as "bad." It's hard to keep up with her. It's a temptation to shout or yell at her to stop rather than get up one more time to take her away from the forbidden object.

Yelling, that's my problem. I don't hit him, but I see him doing something, and right away I yell at him. He gets his feelings hurt real easy.

Anne, 16 - Mark, 16 months

Directions given from a distance are nearly useless.

Don't yell. Get up and walk across the room. Tell him what he should do as you move him away from what he can't have. If you yell your directions from a distance, he probably won't understand them. Even if he does, he's likely to ignore them.

He has little understanding of "right" or "wrong," or what could happen as the result of his actions. He has no idea that the delicate vase he just grabbed could slip out of his hands and break until it has done just that. *Most toddlers are "good" if they happen to feel like doing what they should do and not doing what they should not.*

Actually, young children are neither "good" nor "bad." They are very busy little people learning to do many things. Sometimes the things they do please us, and sometimes they do not. It is the things they *do* that are good or bad. Your child is *never* a bad person!

Independence Becomes Important

Now that she's more able to walk and talk, she feels like a more independent person. She wants to control herself according to her own reasoning, but she lacks the maturity and judgment to do so. Learning to control herself is essential to learning self-control. It's important that you respect her need to demonstrate her independence while you help her live within necessary limits.

> *Mandi got to the Terrible Twos about six months early. She was really independent, and she wanted us to know she was her own person.*
>
> *I probably give her more freedom than Danielle does. When she's outside, we keep an eye on her, but she does pretty well in the yard.*
>
> *What drives me crazy is when she goes out in the street. There's very little traffic here, but she knows she has to take our hand if she's in the street, and she doesn't like doing that. So every evening, if we're out in the yard and I'm not giving her enough attention, she'll go right out there and stand in the gutter and look at me.*
>
> John, 21 - Mandi, 22 months

Support her desire for independence by getting rid of any limits you don't really need. Limits that are needed, such as staying out of the street, *must* be firmly and consistently maintained.

Independence at Bathtime

> *Sonia started saying "No" a week ago. When I start to give her a bath, especially in the morning when I have to take her to school, she runs and says, "No, no." She loves her bath, and I don't know how to handle this.*

*I usually give her choices. If she's doing something
wrong, I move her away and play with her so she'll
forget, or I take her outside. This works a lot better
than yelling at her.*

Estela, 18 - Sonia, 19 months

Estela has the right idea when she says, "I usually give
her choices." Will Sonia accept her bath more pleasantly if
her mother lets her choose which tub toys she takes into the
water? Or perhaps she reacts as she does because her mother is too rushed in the morning. Giving Sonia a bath in the
evening might put less pressure on both Estela and Sonia.

Scribbling and Painting

Your toddler is probably quite curious about your use of
pens and pencils. Now that she can grasp a pencil, she
wants to imitate and scribble, too. If she scribbles in the
wrong places, it becomes a discipline problem.

*A week ago I was taking a bath. I left Sonia here
with all her toys, and she got the crayons and wrote
all over my walls. I laughed, but still I got mad. I
caught her and put her over there with her toys.*

*I told her, "No writing on the walls," and I taped a
paper on her high chair. I said she could write here
but not on the wall.*

*She's too small to know she shouldn't write on the
wall. I'm always putting her in the high chair, and I
take some paper and let her scribble. I'm sure she
thought it was the same thing to write on the wall.*

Estela

Scribbling is the art of toddlers. But what about scribbling on the walls? How would you react if your toddler
practiced her art on the living room walls?

Surely none of us wants scribbling done on our walls. We may have a bulletin board or other way of displaying baby's artwork, but we certainly don't want it on the walls or furniture.

The use of crayons, paints, and other art material is fun for children and helps them express their feelings. Because they are often messy, you'll need to find a suitable place for her to use them. She can work at a table near you while you cook or clean up your kitchen. If you're studying, arrange a place beside you where she can write, too.

While she is still a toddler, a good place for her to scribble is in her high chair. Even when she's older, you'll want her to work with crayons, paint, or other art media in a particular area where clean-up won't be a problem.

Supervision is the key. No one under three should be left in a room by herself with crayons or any other art media. She's too interested in the process of making marks to think about any problems she might be creating. If you're right there, you'll notice when she's ready to write in the wrong place.

You have two choices if you see her walk away from her paper with the crayon still in her hand. You can either bring her back to her paper to crayon some more, or you take the crayon in exchange for another toy.

You might say, "If you want to write, you must write on the paper. If you're through writing, Daddy will take the crayon. Here is your ball."

You need to be careful in choosing the materials she'll use. Since toddlers like to taste everything, all felt pens, paints, and even chalk that you buy should be labeled nontoxic. Pieces of crayons and chalk need to be big enough that she can't choke on them.

She should use pens, pencils, and paint brushes only when she's sitting down. If she falls while walking around with one, she could get a puncture wound.

She'll be ready to try to use scissors by age 2 1/2 or 3. She needs a pair with blunt ends so she won't get hurt.

When you can, use art materials such as finger paints with her. You'll both enjoy it.

What About Biting?

Sometimes two little ones play side by side, generally ignoring each other. At other times they may play together quite happily.

Then suddenly one child is crying, and you see teeth marks on his arm. Someone just got bitten! What should you do?

Some people say, "Bite him back so he'll know how it feels." That's bad advice. He won't understand at all why

Biting is most likely to happen when she's frustrated.

you, the parent he trusts, suddenly bit him and hurt him. Biting him back only shows him that you bite, too.

> *Nicole was a biter for a few weeks. One time the babysitter took her arm and had the other kid bite it. I flipped. I would scold her or remove her, basically the same discipline as if she had hit somebody. I don't believe in the biting back.*
>
> Cara, 24 - Leroy, 8; Paul, 6; Nicole, 5

A young child probably bites for a variety of reasons. Some biting occurs as the result of exploration. He will explore other children as he would objects with touching, hair pulling, mouthing, and biting. He is not aware that biting hurts because he didn't feel any pain.

Teething may also be a cause of biting. The urge to bite must be stronger when teeth are emerging and gums are sore.

A child who can't express himself well with words may discover that biting is an extremely useful way to get his point across. He has learned by experience that if he wants his friend's toy, all he has to do is bite her. She will drop it immediately, and the toy is his.

Naturally you won't allow biting. Tell him firmly that, by biting her, he hurt Janie, and you do not want him to do that. The first bite may be the only one, so don't be too horrified. Be sure he knows you still love him a lot, you just don't accept biting.

If he bites again, remove him from the play area. Tell him he can't be with the other children if he's going to bite. If you have a child who bites time after time, be sure he gets plenty of good attention at other times. Does he bite when he's tired or hungry? You can help him get more rest. Maybe he needs a mid-afternoon snack.

Sometimes a child will bite if the situation has become

too exciting or stressful for him to handle. He may need a quieter place to play or gentler playmates.

Sometimes a child with an older sibling who plays roughly with him will seem to bite quite often. If your child is biting, you may need to limit this sort of play.

"She Hits Me"

> ### Problem
> *Yesterday I took Shannon to the doctor and she wouldn't stand on that thing to be weighed. And she started hitting me. She's 21 months old.*
> "What do you do when she hits you?"
> *It depends. If she hits me for no reason . . .*
>   Calli, 17 - Shannon, 21 months

Young children express frustration in many ways. Hitting may be one. When she hits you, take her hands gently in yours and hold them. Tell her you don't like hitting, and that you don't want her to do that. Tell her in a firm voice that indicates you mean what you say, but don't threaten her.

It's important to recognize her frustration and help her handle it at the same time. Is there a reason for Shannon not wanting to use the scale? Most health professionals are quite considerate of children's feelings, but some are not.

Some children become fearful of the doctor's office because of all the immunizations they must have. Make the visit as pleasant as possible for your child.

When a child hits another child, you respond in much the same way you do if he hits you:

> *He really tests me now. Like this morning, he hit a little girl. I said, "No, Jayme, it's not nice to hit." He hit her again.*

*I sat him down in a chair and I said, "Jayme, no,
that's not nice. You hurt Lisa," and he started crying.*
                                                    Kaylene

Kaylene stayed calm, didn't threaten Jayme, and at the
same time, didn't allow him to hit the other child. He
understood far better than he would have if she had hit him
"to show him what it feels like."

He Will Imitate You

*Manuel follows whatever Leesha does. Leesha has
a little purse with lipstick inside. She uses her finger
to put on her lipstick. Yesterday Manuel had her
purse, and he was putting lipstick all over his finger.
I'm glad we caught him before he got to the walls. He
would have had a great time.*
                                                    Kambria

Your child will often imitate you and others. You're his
model. If he has an older brother or sister, he may mimic
their actions. He learns a lot through imitation.

She will imitate both the things you want her to do *and*
the things you don't want her to do:

*Getting ready to go someplace is a problem. I'll be
trying to put my makeup on, and Elena will come in
and dig through it, then want to smear it on her face.
When she does that, I usually find the lightest color
lipstick I have and let her play with it right there in
front of me.*

*Finally what I did was buy her play makeup. Now
when she sees me putting on mine, she gets hers out.*
                                        Marijane, 18 - Elena, 23 months

Most self-help skills are learned by imitation. The child
wants to learn so she can be more like other family

members. There's nothing wrong with wanting to grow up
and be like mom. Elena is lucky to have a mom who was
able to find a way to deal with the problem in such a
positive way.

Sometimes it's hard to realize your toddler is mimicking
you when she does things you don't like:

> *Cassandra pulls the tapes out from the shelf under
> the TV. I tell her to quit, and she throws the tape. I hit
> her, and finally she tells me she's sorry.*
>
> Kris, 17 - Cassandra, 25 months

When your child is interested in doing things for herself,
she wants to do things that seem important. She sees you
using the tapes, and she doesn't realize she shouldn't do the
same thing. Her intention was not to damage your tapes.
You can't let her tear up your things, of course, but it
doesn't mean she's bad. Rather than hitting her and insist-
ing she say she's sorry, Kris should talk with Cassandra
and explain how fragile the tapes are. She should show
Cassandra the proper way to handle them as she picks them
up. Perhaps Kris could store the tapes in a more secure
place for a few months. Remember our theme — *Make it
easy for your toddler to behave acceptably.*

Telephone Talk for Toddlers

> *She wants all my attention when I'm on the phone.
> One day I was talking to my mom. Elena would get
> the stool, pull it over to the desk, and climb up on the
> desk. I kept getting her down and moving the stool,
> and she'd bring it back again. Finally, when I was
> trying to help her, she fell against the desk and got
> hurt. It's like you tell them and tell them, but she
> doesn't listen, and she finally learns.*
>
> Marijane

Using the phone helps her learn to use language.

Many toddlers will be fussy and whiny if mother is on the telephone. Others will cause an amazing amount of mischief. It's difficult for many children to have mother be so close but inaccessible.

He can see her, hear her, and possibly even touch her, but someone else has her attention. A toddler has a difficult time sharing his mother's attention. By misbehaving, he knows he's likely to get it back. He would rather have negative attention than none at all.

> *She loves to talk on the phone, and that's another problem. When I let her, she doesn't want to give it back to me. Finally she'll get her play phone and act like she's talking on it.*
>
> *I usually let her answer the phone. Sometimes she'll give it to me, and sometimes she won't. If it's a*

*voice she doesn't know, she'll give it to me right
away. If she recognizes the voice, especially if it's
grandma, she'll talk all day.*

Marijane

If he's allowed to use the phone, too, he may be a little
more patient during his mother's phone call, especially if
it's a short call.

Using the telephone will also aid in language development. On the phone he'll be unable to use gestures, and
he'll have to find words to express his thoughts. It's nice if
an interested, caring person will talk and listen to your
child on the phone.

Saying "Bad" Words

Problem

*Kamie's been saying a bad word. First, it was
funny. But then, when we'd take her places, she still
said the "f" word. It's not funny now.*

*She says it with a b instead of f — "Buck you!"
When she gets on the phone, the first thing she says to
her grandma is, "Buck you!" What do we do?*

Kelsey, 19 - Kamie, 21 months

Kamie has no idea at this stage of the meaning of the "f"
word. She's learning to talk, and most of the time, her
parents, grandma, and others are pleased and excited with
each new word she uses.

This time, she got a different reaction. But she did get a
reaction, a strong one. First, they laughed, and that made it
worth her while to say the word over and over again. Now
they don't like it, but she still gets attention when she
says it.

If a child this young uses words you don't think are
appropriate, usually the best strategy is to ignore it. When

she's a little older, you can quietly explain, "We don't use that word. Please don't say it any more." But at Kamie's age, she's more likely to forget it if her parents (and her grandma) ignore the situation.

The real solution, of course, is to be very sure that, at least when she's around you and the rest of her family, she never hears words you don't want her to repeat. Give her a model you want her to mimic.

You Can Model Manners

Do you want your child to say "Thank you" and "Please" at the table or other appropriate times? The best way is not to order her to say those magic words or even ask her to repeat them. She's not a parrot. But remember how much she likes to imitate you? If she hears you using those words, she'll use them, too.

Appreciate Your Child!

As your child becomes more and more independent, you may become more concerned about discipline. Continue to set only necessary limits and to enforce those limits firmly. Continue to keep your child's environment as safe and open to exploration as you can.

If you treat your child with respect and give him lots of positive attention, you may find this early independence stage goes smoothly. You will continue enjoying your child because, thanks to all your efforts, most of the time he probably behaves fairly well.

Appreciate him and have fun with him!

He learns through positive teaching, not from yelling and hitting.

6

Yelling, Spanking Don't Help

- **Being Yelled at Hurts Him**
- **Parenting Isn't Easy**
- **Your Feelings Count**
- **Must Children Be Hit, Slapped, or Spanked?**
- **"No Hitting in Here"**
- **Spanking Doesn't Help**
- **Punishment Interferes with Learning**
- **Helping Your Toddler Behave**
- **Setting Limits with Respect**

If we just remember to treat them as "small people," like being polite to them. Yelling at them all the time can be just as wrong as abusing them physically.

Thelma, 20 - Melissa, 4;
Janeen, 18 months

Dalton is past 21/2 and he's very rowdy, non-stop. He has so much energy from the time he wakes up at 6 until he goes to bed at 8:30 or 9. He loves attention. He's very cuddly at times.

Dalton went through a NO stage. His answer to everything was "No" for the longest

*time. He could be hungry, and he would say "No"
when we asked him to come eat.*

*I was spanked as a kid, and I didn't like it. It taught
me to be afraid when a hand got raised or when
somebody's voice got loud because usually when I got
spanked it was when someone was yelling.*

*It didn't help me behave, and I honestly don't think
it would help Dalton. Talking to him seems to
work better.*

                                        Claire, 17 - Dalton, 33 months

Being Yelled at Hurts Him

*I don't yell. I just hold his hand, and I tell him,
"No." I don't yell because I see this one girl yell. Her
son is younger than mine, and he's freaked out about
it. He doesn't understand.*

                                        Grechelle, 16 - MacKenzie, 11 months

No one should ever discipline a child in anger. Too often
in anger, people use tactics they would never want their
child to copy. They're rude. They yell, they use bad
language, and they make horrible threats.

*People think child abuse is beating your kid. But
it's not just that. It's also yelling at them. That's what
really hurts the kid because they don't know what
you're saying, and they do it again, and they get hit
for it.*

*You yell, and they don't understand. They're
frustrated, and you get frustrated. They start getting
into trouble more and more.*

                                        Roseanna, 14 - Felipe, 2

Yelling is verbal abuse. It is frightening to a child. It's
hard on his self-esteem. Poor self-esteem is a nasty stum-
bling block not only to good behavior, but to learning as

well. If he feels he isn't a good person, he won't act like one. That's not what you want for your child.

We are our children's models. If we want our children to respect other people, we have to show respect for them. We must demonstrate the behavior we want them to imitate.

Parenting Isn't Easy

Being a parent of an active, inventive, curious young child is not an easy task. In spite of all your good intentions to do otherwise, there may be a time when you do yell at her about what she's done.

She'll be frightened when you do, but, hopefully, you'll soon get back in control of yourself. It will be over within a few minutes, and you'll be ready to talk and play with her again. Of course it's important that it doesn't happen often.

I try. I'm better now. There for awhile I was losing patience and I'd yell at Carlos, tell him to shut up.

I have a temper, but I can take more now than I could before.

Renette, 16 - Carlos, 6 months

Just remember that she may have no idea why you suddenly screamed at her. She can't possibly understand that grabbing the plant one more time was the last straw. You simply couldn't take any more without yelling.

Try to explain to her what happened. Tell her you're sorry you yelled at her. You can admit that you were very angry, and that you just don't have enough patience today.

I'm a short-fused person, and I don't have a lot of patience. When I'm upset with my mom or with Julio, I always seem to take it out on the kids.

I'm beginning to realize it isn't my kids' fault. I've learned to talk more because Alina likes it more when

I sit and talk to her and tell her why this is wrong.
When I yell at her, she puts her arms up to shield her
face — even though I haven't spanked her real hard. I
tell her, "Alina, don't do that. Momma's not going to
hit you."

I told Julio the other day that we need to talk to the
kids more. They don't want to be yelled at. It just goes
in one ear and out the other, and it's damaging. The
more I sit and talk to them, the better they do.

This morning Alina spilled her juice. She just
looked at me and thought I'd yell at her. I told her it
was okay, and when she was done eating, I'd give her
a drink. But it's hard to be patient.

Joanne, 23 - Francene, 4 1/2; Alina, 3; Gloria, 1

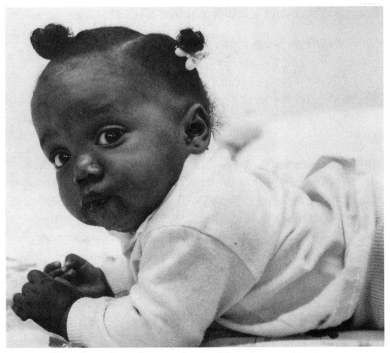

She doesn't understand why Mom is upset today.

Your Feelings Count

How you feel about yourself influences how you discipline your child. If your life is going well today, you probably aren't going to take your frustrations out on your child. If he spills his milk on the floor when you're rested and feeling really good, how do you react?

What if he spills his milk right after your partner calls to say he's working late again and you can't go out tonight? Or you've just learned your boyfriend is leaving town? Is there a difference in how you respond to your toddler's messiness? If there is, you're normal.

If I'm sick or get a headache, it isn't Marty's fault that he's acting normal. If I don't feel like running around watching him, sometimes I go take a bath. He'll take it with me or sit next to me with his toys. That relaxes both of us.

Yumiko, 16 - Marty, 21 months

Realizing this happens and not feeling guilty about it is a good place to start. Sometimes even with a toddler, it's best simply to tell him you're upset today. Assure him it's not his fault. Then hug him an extra time. Of course you'll still have to be extra careful not to take your angry feelings out on your child.

Sometimes Meghan will do things that bother me a lot, and I know I have to get her away from me for awhile. When my mom's there, I go outside for awhile. There's always a day when your nerves are on edge and you have to get out for awhile. I thought it was just me, but it isn't.

Once I pushed her away, and she fell and bit her tongue. I felt so bad. I hugged her and said, "Mommy is feeling bad today." She seemed to understand.

Louise, 19 - Meghan, 23 months; Mark, 5 months

All parents get upset with their kids, even their babies. But if it gets to the point where you're yelling at and hitting your child because of your own frustrations, think about getting help. See chapter 12 for suggestions.

Must Children Be Hit, Slapped, or Spanked?

When she was younger, I used to stick her in her room. Then the older she got, if it was something bad, I'd smack her butt.

Then I don't know what happened, but one day it clicked that I shouldn't have been doing that. So now I count to 3, and she'll straighten up. I don't smack her any more.

One day she was crying, and she said, "Mom hurt me." I never hit her hard, just a swat on the diaper, but I couldn't do that any more.

Madge, 18 - Destiny, 3

Should children be slapped or spanked? Some people say, "Yes," but more and more people are saying "No." Usually they say "No" because they have discovered that spanking doesn't work very well. Hitting a child won't make her be obedient. There's no way you can force her to eat or to urinate in the toilet, for example.

Spankings generally lead to more and harder spankings to make the child respond. Children handled in this way are more likely to get into fights and other difficulties as they get older. Spanking is not a satisfactory way to force compliance.

You start spanking them, and they're going to learn the bad part of life, the violent side. I wouldn't spank because I used to be spanked and it wasn't fun. And it made me worse.

Debra, 16 - Nicholas, 4 weeks

"No Hitting in Here"

Problem

Yesterday in the Infant Center Victor went over to an eight-month-old girl. He pulled her hair real hard and was growling at her. I went over and slapped his hand and said, "No, Victor, no."

The teacher saw me, and she said crossly, "No hitting in here."

I told her this is my baby, and I just patted his hand and told him "No." That upset me for the whole day. She acted like I was murdering him, and everybody was looking.

Raylene, 18 - Victor, 2

It's not the childcare worker's intention to embarrass a parent. In a child development center state regulations don't allow any adult to punish a child physically. The caregiver must stop even parents from spanking or slapping children. It's their job.

Their job is to teach. They are trying to demonstrate other ways of handling children that will have a better chance for continued success. They want to help make your task as a parent less difficult and less frustrating.

Professional caregivers who work with many young children in a group never spank them. They seldom have problems.

They know that if they have realistic expectations for behavior based on the age and development of the children, and they treat the children with respect, there will be few problems.

Childcare workers try to help parents learn to treat their children in the same manner. Childrearing based on love and respect is much more enjoyable for both the parent and the child.

Spanking Doesn't Help

I think some people use spanking too much. I have
a lot of friends, and when we were growing up, I was
fairly good, but I had friends who were getting the
belt every other day for what they did. I think that just
made them more spiteful. They would tell me how they
hated their fathers because they hit them.

                                                            Yumiko

Think of the children you know who are spanked. Do
they behave well? We remember a young mother in our
parenting class who insisted that children *must* be spanked.
"I have these two nephews," she said. "They're terrible,
and their parents *have* to spank them all the time."

"Does the spanking help?" we asked. "Are they
behaving well now?"

She thought for a minute, then said, "Well, no . . . I
guess it hasn't helped them at all."

Punishment tells a child what not to do in a hurting,
painful way. He still doesn't know what he should have
done instead. Left with resentment and anger, he may not
even care. The offense will most likely be repeated again.
The real lesson taught is not to get caught.

It is the work of children to explore and learn. It is the
job of parents to encourage, teach, and make exploring
safe. Spanking makes exploration and learning risky,
not safe.

Spanking or slapping a child is not a good idea for many
reasons. The baby or toddler will seldom understand why
you, someone he trusts, hit him to make him cry. Even if he
realizes that he displeased you, he now knows that hurting
people is all right, especially if you're bigger and stronger.
It must be — daddy or mother hit him. It's all right to
be a bully!

I don't think spanking is necessary. It's just teaching them that a big person can hit a little person. I think kids are more likely to think it's okay to hit if they've been hit.

Zandra, 16 - Dakota, 11 months

A child who has been slapped or spanked is likely to grow into an angry teenager who gets into fights and has other difficulties. These same angry feelings may carry into adulthood to cause more problems.

Parents should demonstrate the behaviors they want their child to copy. A child who experiences understanding and respect from his parents is more likely to treat others in the same way.

She learns fear when her parents yell at her or spank her.

*I just started saying "No," and it crushes Jayme. I
don't like doing that, but I know he has to have
discipline.*

*I don't believe in spanking . . . I think it's just a
form of child abuse to tell you the truth. Kids can do
some bad things, but they're still children.*

*I don't even believe in spanking a child who is five
years old. Spanking just causes more problems. I
wasn't spanked, and I'm kind of following my
mother's footsteps on discipline.*

Kaylene, 18 - Jayme, 16 months

Punishment Interferes with Learning

Punishment tries to control behavior by force, using pain
and loss for effectiveness. It can interfere with learning
because none of us learns as well when we're afraid.
Punishment too often gives a child a feeling of failure.

*You're closer to the one that doesn't spank you. I
did what my dad said because he never hit me. Hitting
isn't going to help anyway because you get hit and it's
over. It don't make any difference.*

Wayne, 17 - Ricky, 6 months

Harsh punishment is emotionally scarring. While some
children seek revenge, others become guilty and humiliated
victims, people afraid to do anything for fear of failure.
They don't learn to think for themselves.

Blind obedience is not the goal of discipline. Blind
obedience will cause a child to be a follower who will do
what other people tell her to do without judging whether
it's right or wrong.

Another reason not to use hitting as punishment is the
real danger of getting out of control. Physical child abuse is
a tragic reality for many families in the United States. More

than a million children are abused each year, and about 2,000 die from child abuse. See chapter 12.

My mom said once I was doing something really terrible. She spanked me, and she got to the point where she knew she had to stop. She realized that she would hurt me. At that moment she knew how somebody could be a child abuser.

You just have to make yourself stop. If you start hitting a little bit and it doesn't work, you're going to start hitting harder. If a kid doesn't get hit, it will work better.

Yumiko

If a parent decides that hitting is a good method of punishment, that parent may be more likely to hit too hard than would the parent who doesn't believe in hitting in the first place. Parents who were spanked a lot or physically abused as children are more likely to abuse their children.

Helping Your Toddler Behave

I try talking to Jamaica first. I don't push the spanking or the hitting thing. Spanking is not appropriate, and I don't think it's right. If you spank them every time they get into something . . . she's just curious, and I don't want to spank her.

I think Jamaica understands my words better than she understands spanking. Once I spanked her hand, and she turned around and spanked her doll and said "No!" I knew right then that talking with her would work better than that.

Kyli, 17 - Jamaica, 22 months

You can, and should, limit your toddler with necessary restrictions. You can, and should, stop his activities when

necessary either by removing him from the scene or helping him do what he must do. It is part of your job as
his parent.

Many parents resort to an occasional swat on a diapered
bottom. Their child survives nicely, but the fact remains,
that swat probably didn't accomplish much. A child who is
spanked is actually less likely to obey his parents in
the future.

*Felipe does something bad, like getting in the
refrigerator over and over in the middle of the night.
Sometimes I'll spank him.*

*He'll cry for about five minutes, then go right back
to the refrigerator. But if I tell him to go to bed, and
in the morning he can have Cheerios, he'll go back to
bed without a spanking.*

                                                    Roseanna

If you find you're spanking your child a great deal, is it
possible he doesn't get much of your attention otherwise?
How much time do you spend playing with him and giving
him your full attention? How often do you praise him when
he's behaving well? Boys are less likely than girls to get
this kind of positive attention. Love and trust your child,
and let him know you do.

*I don't believe in spanking unless they do some-
thing life-threatening or hurt someone else. I find
taking a favorite toy away or sending them to their
room is more effective.*

*The most important thing is to make sure you let
them know when they do something good. It's more
fun for them to be happy rather than sad. Also let
them know they're part of your life, not just kids living
in your home. They do make a difference.*

                           Cara, 24 - Leroy, 8; Paul, 6; Nicole, 5

Setting Limits with Respect

How I compromise with Lorenzo is talk to him about how he feels about the situation. He knows we're in charge.

If he doesn't obey, I ask him why he doesn't listen to me. He's really never given us a problem. We never spank him —I never thought that was right. I was spanked, and I didn't appreciate it, and I sure didn't learn from it. I just got mad. Spanking doesn't do the job. What are they learning from you spanking them? Just that big people hurt little people.

I never liked the way I was brought up. I would never want to put my son through that. Abusing your child is the worst thing you can ever do. Why would you ever hit your child? He'd despise you. You're supposed to be someone they look up to, and you're sitting there hitting him.

Lorenzo is a sensitive, gentle kid, perhaps because he's never been abused or hit.

Guadalupe, 20 - Lorenzo, 4

You can discipline your child more effectively without hitting or yelling. Setting limits with respect works better.

You have to stay thoughtful as a parent. You have to stay ahead of the kids. Perhaps you have to block out the time to stand back and figure out how your child feels and why he behaves the way he does.

Taking time for this kind of thinking is a good start toward planning discipline strategies that work without yelling, slapping, or hitting. When you do, *both you and your child can win.*

She wants to help you with your important jobs.

7

Two to Three Years — Your Busy Runabout

Leah takes her clothes off by herself, but she doesn't put them on. Usually I let her pick out what she wants to wear. I put out two outfits and let her pick one. Sometimes when I haven't done that and I just put something on her, she won't wear it, and I have to change it.

You need to say, "Which one do you want?" instead of "What do you want?" I've tried giving her three choices, but sometimes that confuses her, so usually I just give her two.

You have to compromise

with toddlers. Everything can't be your way. I take
into consideration what Leah wants, and sometimes I
go halfway. We respect her.

Lyra, 18 - Leah, 2½

"I'll Do It Myself"

I kept waiting for the Terrible Twos. But it's not as
bad as I expected. We try to talk to him. We'd rather
talk to him than hit. Why hit?

When my brothers and I were disciplined, my mom
and dad would look at us, get good eye contact, and
say, "Look what you did wrong. Don't do it again."

Dustin is attentive and bright, and if you tell him
with a serious tone to get his attention, he hears us.

Mark, 22 - Dustin, 2½

Young children develop and learn so quickly that you'll
notice changes in your child almost continually. Your two-
to three-year-old is busily learning new words and is more
able to talk.

She will usually understand what you tell her if you use
simple words and short phrases. There will be many times,
however, when she doesn't understand the meaning of your
comments and directions. To her, words generally have
very simple meanings and uses. She has just barely begun
to learn about language.

Often when a toddler seems to be behaving defiantly,
she simply doesn't understand how she's expected to act.
You can help her if, before speaking to her, you stoop
down and get eye contact with her. Now you have her
attention. Talk to her slowly and use words you know she
understands.

At around two years, a child is able to do many things by
himself. It's important that he begin to learn how to take
care of some of his own needs. The development of

self-help skills isn't always easy for the parent.

He's more able to feed himself. He will try to wash his hands and face and brush his hair. He may even want to brush his own teeth.

He's beginning to undress himself, and he tries to put some of his clothes back on. About this time he may begin to express definite ideas about the clothes he's willing to wear:

> *Felicia is at the stage where she wants to take her clothes off. She takes her shoes off and her shirt. She won't sleep in pajamas. She sleeps in her panties or diaper and a tee shirt. What can I do about that?*
>
> Antoinette, 18 - Felicia, 2½

If you can go along with her clothing desires, do so. A warm tee shirt and a diaper are probably just as good as pajamas. It's nice for a toddler to have some control. At this young age, she has to conform so often to the commands of others.

She is quite proud of her new skills, but she's slow, clumsy, and easily frustrated. She may refuse your help one minute, and then cry the next because you aren't helping her. She's learning a lot, but you'll need to help her in subtle ways so that she can enjoy success.

Helping your child perform these tasks will take much more time than if you simply did them yourself. However, your patient help and guidance will enable her to feel competent and able to learn even more skills. This is an important part of your teaching job.

Elena is showing her independence through wanting to be alone occasionally. Her father commented:

> *Elena's very independent. Sometimes it scares me. At this age, I wonder how she'll be when she's a*

teenager.

When she started this, it got my attention. I would sit there and think, "Oh my god." I would go in her room, and she would literally grab me by the hand and lead me out, then close the door.

Or she would get mad at us and go in and close the door because she wanted to be alone. I guess that's okay. Her room is a safe place, and I can understand wanting to be alone. Sometimes I feel that way.

Raul, 19 - Elena, 23 months

Raul is showing respect for his daughter's feelings. That's an important part of discipline.

"Who's in Charge?"

Problem

She's a holy terror. She gets into everything. We're having a battle over who's in charge. She tries to make it so she's in charge rather than Mommy. She's into everything. Being a single parent is real hard.

Cathi, 18 - Susie, 34 months

Cathi needs to set the limits and consistently maintain them, but Susie should be allowed to be in charge of some of her life. At this young age, she'll have to conform to many rules she really doesn't understand. Letting her be in charge when it doesn't matter is okay.

If Cathi allows Susie some freedom, she's likely to behave better. At the same time, at 34 months, she still needs a great deal of attention from her mother. Sometimes a parent, especially a single parent, is so busy that it's hard to spend blocks of time solely with her child(ren). Having more of mother's undivided attention might help Susie be less of a "holy terror."

The Helper

Young children love to imitate. Your child has spent many hours watching you. Many of the jobs you do around the house look interesting to him. Now he may want to help you.

He likes to do things that produce results that he can see and understand. He may try to help you dust. If you have a short broom, he'll help you sweep. He may want to set the table or remove the dishes at the end of a meal. Using plastic dishes that are lighter for him to carry and which won't break easily will make his "job" go better for him.

He's slow and awkward when he helps, but he wants to be useful. These jobs are important to him. Through imitation, he's trying to get an idea of what it will feel like to be grown up.

It may be an entirely different situation if there is a task you want him to do. Sometimes he will be delightfully cooperative, but at other times he can be exasperating and difficult.

Working him is genera. much more

Sometimes he wants to help.

effective than giving directions. If you want him to pick up
his toys, don't order, "Pick up your toys right now." Instead, make it a game. You might suggest he put his toys in
his wagon. Tell him you'll help him haul them to the toy
shelves.

You'll be able to think of lots of other ways to get him to
want to do what you want him to do. This is so much more
important than setting out to prove to him that he "must"
obey you. A battle of wills results in lots of frustration for
both of you, and little else.

Setting a good example is extremely important. If you
want your child to pick up his toys, you can't leave your
things all over the house. If everyone around him is fairly
neat, your child is more likely to be neat.

When I (Jeanne) visited Annabel, her 5- and 7-year-old
children were playing with puzzles on the living room floor
while we talked. After awhile, they picked everything up
without even being asked. Annabel explained:

I learned from training my husband. He grew up
not having to put things away, and I didn't want that.
If the children get out a game, the first one is picked
up before they get another one. Even my two-year-old,
if he gets out a wooden puzzle, has to put it away
before he can get another one.

They learn by example. If I use something, I clean
up and put it away when I'm done. If we play a game,
we put it away when we're through.

I think you have to start when they're young. Once
they start playing with things with pieces, it's time to
start cleaning up what they have.

There are times when they can't play a game. If
they play it today and don't put it away, they can't
play it again this week.

Annabel, 27 - Andrew, 10; Anthony, 7; Bianca, 5; James, 2

"She's Looking for Attention"

Problem

Alina gets real jealous because Francine goes to school plus I have a baby who gets all my attention. Alina tends to pick on the baby, pull her hair. She's in the middle, and she gets real upset and tries to pick on Gloria. I think she's looking for attention. She holds her little pillow and sucks her thumb a lot.

The hardest thing has been Francene starting school and Alina can't go. She says, "I want to go to school, I want a backpack."

Francene comes home and says, "Mommy, guess what we did," and she's excited. Alina cuts right in and tries to mimic her. Francene brings home a picture and Alina immediately brings out a picture she made.

Joanne, 23 - Francene, 4 1/2; Alina, 3; Gloria, 1

Alina may feel cheated because she doesn't feel she gets enough of her mother's attention. She sees her mother taking care of the baby and Francene getting attention for her schoolwork. No wonder Alina tries to be involved, too.

Perhaps Joanne could have "school" for Alina at home in the mornings. She could plan activities for Alina while she does her housework.

Perhaps each day Alina could do something special like finger painting. Reading books together and drawing pictures about the stories would be fun. Of course Alina's drawings should be displayed along with Francene's school work. Joanne might find Alina actually taking less of her time if she started providing more activities for her.

Another interesting part of those activities could be letting Alina "help" her mother with the cleaning.

Joanne is concerned that Alina needs more attention.

Looking back, she wishes she had spaced her children further apart. "Alina never had much of a chance to be a baby," she commented wistfully. If you agree with Joanne that children need a lot of attention, you may decide to delay having another baby for awhile.

Not Ready to Share

We're having a problem in the nursery. Larissa's not used to being around other kids so sharing is hard for her. If somebody has something she wants, she will pull hair or scratch. It's hard teaching her not to do that.

                                        Leila, 18 - Larissa, 21/2

Larissa, at age 21/2, is not yet able to use words to get the things she wants. She needs adult help to understand that her friend is using the toy now and she really needs to wait until he's through. While she's waiting, she should be given another interesting toy to examine.

Young children aren't ready to share toys. They're too busy learning what is "mine" to understand about sharing.

Robin is stingy. She'll have all her toys laid out, and she won't be playing with them. But if somebody else comes, she's ornery and won't share at all.

I have a nephew who is 21/2. Robin beats him up, pulls his hair, bites him and takes his toys away. He does the same thing back to her. Or he cries, "Robin hit me."

                                        Melinda, 16 - Robin, 19 months

Occasionally a toddler will offer a toy to another child, but she will quite likely demand it be returned immediately. If it's not returned, she'll either grab it back quickly or cry from rage and frustration. Robin, her cousin, and Larissa

Sometimes big brother is willing to play with her.

are behaving normally for their ages. An adult needs to be nearby who will patiently help them interact more constructively. This is how they can begin to learn social skills.

Interacting with Siblings

Adam likes to tease Cami. He'll hold her feet down so she can't crawl. He'll stick his socks in her face. When she's on the couch, he'll move her hands so she'll fall off.

It's as if sometimes he likes to make her cry. He'll tease her, hide something she has. He'll yell when we're talking. How can we get him to treat Cami nicely?

Leona, 18 - Adam, 4; Cami, 1

Adam is having trouble with sibling rivalry (feeling of being displaced by younger sister or brother). He hasn't really accepted Cami yet. Whenever these two are together, an adult will need to be near. As Cami gets bigger, they may begin to enjoy some activities together. But until Adam understands he can't hurt Cami, they'll need adult supervision and separate play spaces.

> *I have three brothers living here and Celeste bugs them. One is six, and he goes, "She's getting into this," and "She's getting into that."*
> *Celeste is real rough with Carrie. She has a bad temper, and when we tell her "No," she screams. I don't know why she's like that. I sit down with her, I color with her, I read with her, but I have to spend time with both of them.*
> Noelle-Marie, 19 - Celeste, 2 1/2; Carrie, 9 months

Celeste is truly a middle child. She is too young to play with the older brothers. No matter how much she pesters them, they won't accept her. And now her mother is busy with her younger sister and has far less time to be Celeste's playmate. Celeste, too, may have feelings of sibling rivalry. Celeste might be happier if she could play with children closer to her age, either in a preschool or with other neighborhood children. She seems to be seeking a playmate.

Jealous of New Baby

Often, a small child is quite jealous of a new baby. He feels displaced by this new person who takes so much of mom's and dad's attention. Why should he be thrilled? He can't play with the baby. The baby only cries and sleeps. Mom may always seem to be holding the baby instead of him. If baby finally goes to sleep, mom needs to sleep, too. No wonder the displaced toddler often feels resentment:

> *Ricardo is jealous of Monique because she's younger. If we hug Monique, he wants to be hugged,*

*too. When I'm talking to Monique, he will move
between us because he wants attention.*

*When Monique was born he was jealous. He had a
time when he cried so much. Almost anything would
get him to crying. I think it was because of Monique.
He still wants everything that Monique gets.*

Sharon, 19 - Ricardo, 35 months; Monique, 16 months

Rashion observed the jealousy Athenea felt when
Enrique was born:

*It's hard having a small child, then having another,
and trying to take care of both. You have to be very
stable, and you have to have a strict budget.*

*There was a lot of jealousy when Enrique was
born. I would tell Athenea this is not only my child.
This is our baby, and we have to take care of this
baby together.*

*That helped a lot because she stopped seeing
Enrique as her brother, and instead as her baby. I'd
let her hold the baby, and I'd show her how.*

Rashion, 20 - Athenea, 3; Enrique, 22 months

Remember Your Needs, Too

It's important that you give your child lots of attention.
You set only the necessary limits, and you're consistent
about enforcing those limits.

While you're trying to be as positive as possible in your
approach to him, what are you doing for yourself? It's also
important that you meet some of your own needs.

Are you spending some time away from your child? Are
you able to make time to enjoy yourself at least occasionally? Parents who are satisfied with their own lives usually
are able to be more positive with their children.

Both you and your child are important!

She isn't enjoying her tantrum any more than you are.

8

Dealing with Child's Temper Tantrum

- *Why* Does She Have Temper Tantrums?
- Help Him Understand His Feelings
- Making Time for Your Child
- Supermarket Discipline
- Interacting with Siblings

Oh yes, Jeremy has tantrums. Not real bad, but sometimes he's on the floor screaming his head off and kicking. I say, "Stop and listen to me," but he won't listen. I leave him there until he comes to me himself. He does this to get his way when I tell him, "No, you can't have it."

Ernesta, 20 - Jeremy, 3;
Osvaldo, Jr., 5 months

When Shelly gets really mad, she holds her breath, and I'm afraid she might pass out one of these days.

She started when she was ten months old. She turns

purple. I blow in her face and she breathes again.
Sometimes I scold her. Then I start hugging her
because I know she's upset.

Dixie, 18 - Shelly, 17 months

Why Does She Have Temper Tantrums?

Most of the time your discipline techniques will probably work quite well with your toddler. Sooner or later, however, a temper tantrum may occur. Some toddlers have more tantrums than others.

Temper tantrums happen because of frustration. During this stage, your child will have a lot of negative feelings. He wants so badly to do everything himself. But when he tries to put his clothes on, it's a struggle. Or he tries to put a big can into a little one, and it doesn't work. Yet he doesn't want you to help him.

These and many more happenings add up to a lot of frustration, but he can't talk it out. He doesn't know many words yet so he screams. His screaming may turn into a real out-of-control temper tantrum.

The tantrum is an expression of his feelings of anger and frustration and his inability to cope. His feelings are sincere and strong. He is enraged and absolutely miserable. He has lost control of his behavior and may be very difficult to handle.

Losing control — in the form of frequent tantrums — can be pretty frightening for him. He desperately wants to do things his way. At the same time, he needs your firm guidance.

What Can You Do?

What should you do? First, what should you *not* do? Don't spank or otherwise punish your already upset child. If he's having a "real" tantrum, he's lost control of his own actions. If he's "just" screaming, hitting him won't help, and it surely will not stop his screaming.

Don't give in to him either. If he's screaming because you said he couldn't have a piece of candy, don't stop the screaming by handing over the candy. If you do, what happens next time he wants candy? You have another screaming session.

How you respond to his tantrums now will affect his actions in the future. If he finds that having a tantrum means he'll get what he wants, he will act on that learning and use a tantrum as a technique for getting his own way.

On the other hand, if his parent screams at him, perhaps hits him to "give him something to cry about," his frustrations will continue to build. He learns that his parents may not be people he can turn to when he needs help.

He's less likely to become the self-confident, problem-solving, coping individual you'd like him to be. Instead, he needs to learn better ways of managing his life. You can help him by staying calm and loving when he has a tantrum. Noelle-Marie has a wonderful response to Celeste when Celeste is upset:

> *When Celeste has a tantrum, I say, "Come here, let me hold you and love you." It helps her calm down.*
> Noelle-Marie, 19 - Celeste, 2½; Carrie, 9 months

When your child has a tantrum, a good approach, if possible, may be holding him gently. Feeling the security of your arms may have a calming effect. After all, he is a very upset little child, and he needs to know you still love him — even though you won't give in to his demands.

Help Him Understand His Feelings

You can help him if you first recognize how he feels and then verbalize his feelings. Tell him you're sorry that he's so upset and angry. Then try to help him calm down.

This does not mean that you give in to his demands. It may mean holding him securely but gently. Or perhaps you can find other ways to help him regain control of himself, such as a quiet place to rest. He isn't enjoying the tantrum any more than you are.

When he has quieted, talk to him about his feelings. Are there other ways he could handle the situation? With your help he will learn to recognize, control, and deal with his anger in a more positive way.

You won't be able to prevent all temper outbursts. However, you may be able to eliminate some of the reasons he's having tantrums.

> *Genny has tantrums over the car keys. She'll have my keys, and I'll say I have to go, and I take them. She'll throw herself down and start screaming. I think I'll buy her a keyholder with fake keys that will look like my Bart Simpson holder.*
>
> Miguel, 18 - Genny, 18 months

Miguel is wise to figure out a way to eliminate the *cause* of Genny's tantrums.

Barbara Hellstrom, one of the illustrators for *Your Pregnancy and Newborn Journey,* offered to get a photo of her eighteen-month-old daughter, Sara, having a tantrum. Sara cooperated several times — until Barbara showed up with her camera. At that point, Sara would decide it was time to stop her tantrum. Perhaps we've discovered a great truth — pointing a camera at a child is an effective way to stop tantrums.

Actually, the camera probably diverted Sara from thinking about whatever was causing her tantrum. Her mother's attention in this positive way helped Sara regain control of herself.

Sometimes it's tough being a child.

Making Time for Your Child

Arranging your own time schedule so you have extra time for dealing with your toddler is one effective step toward good discipline. Some toddlers tend to have temper tantrums when they're not receiving the attention they want.

> *Vanessa has tantrums real bad. She doesn't when we're alone, but when company is here, or dad's home or grandma, then she does. She hates it when no one pays attention to her. She'll bug you and bug you.*
> Rene, 18 - Vanessa, 19 months; Shavone, 1 month

Tantrums may come at the worst times when you are the busiest and have no extra time to cope with them. She may have a tantrum when you're trying to get ready for school on time or you must get dinner on the table for your family.

Could it be because you're rushing, and you aren't responding to your child's needs? Sometimes an extra ten minutes would allow you and your toddler to do what you feel you have to do without both of you feeling frantic.

Problem

Shelly drives me nuts sometimes. When I'm in a rush to do something, I have to get her ready in a hurry. Sometimes she starts crying, and I really get mad.

Dixie, 18 - Shelly, 17 months

If it's time to get ready for school and your child "refuses" to let you dress her, you don't need to hit her or scream at her. Instead, distract her by giving her a toy or picture book to look at while you get dressed.

If that doesn't work, you can say, "I'm sorry you're upset, but I have to dress now so we can go to school." When you're dressed, if she continues to yell and jump up and down, tell her, "It's too bad you feel so angry, but you need to get dressed now." Hold her firmly, but gently, and dress her. If you can be calm, friendly, and caring, you will probably get her dressed faster than if you hit her or yelled at her. That would only prolong the tantrum.

Be sure she knows you love and respect her even if you don't like what she's doing. Don't ever attack her personally. Attack what she is *doing,* not her. For example, tell her, "You're making it very difficult for me to get ready for school. I'm getting really frustrated."

Supermarket Discipline

If we're at the store and Elena wants out of the basket, she throws a fit. We can't do anything about

*it, so I usually pick her up and walk her around. If
Marijane goes to the store, she usually leaves Elena
with me. That's a lot easier. If we both go, we try to
work together with her.*

Raul, 19 - Elena, 23 months

The supermarket is one of the more difficult places to
handle children. You are there to shop, but your child may
be overwhelmed by the wondrous view of objects to explore. Unfortunately, the market is not child safe. Instead it
is set up with bright colors to attract attention to the very
things she shouldn't touch.

*When we take Dalton to the grocery store, we
usually bring small toys for him — and he knows he'll
get a cookie if he doesn't misbehave. If he does
misbehave, he goes out to the car with his father, and
he doesn't get to ride the horsie.*

Claire 17 - Dalton, 33 months

Practicing good discipline skills with other people
watching is not easy.

*When Olivia sees a toy at the store, she says, "I
want that, I want that."*

*I say, "No, Olivia, we don't have enough money.
We have to get food."*

*She'll arch her back and try to run from me. She
won't get in the seat. Eventually I divert her to
something else.*

Jacquie, 23 - Gabriella, 7; Olivia, 4

Has your child ever thrown a tantrum at the supermarket? Did you handle it the same way you would have if
you'd been home? Or did you feel you "had" to punish him
because of what other people might think if you didn't?

It's a temptation to change the rules when people are

watching. We all want to be considered "good" parents.
Even if we know it doesn't help to scold or hit a toddler in
the middle of a tantrum, we may feel people around us
think we should. Or we may do the opposite — give him
the cookie, or whatever started the tantrum. Anything to
turn off his embarrassing yelling.

Treat your child's supermarket tantrum the same way
you handle a tantrum at home. Be calm and reasonable, but
don't give in to his demands.

> *Paul was the worst tantrum thrower. He'd throw
> himself down and act like I was beating him in the
> store. I'd try to pick him up, and he'd throw himself
> out of my arms. I'd say, "Your crying is not going to
> help, and it's going to be even longer before you can
> have what you want."*
>
> Cara, 24 - Leroy, 8; Paul, 6; Nicole, 5

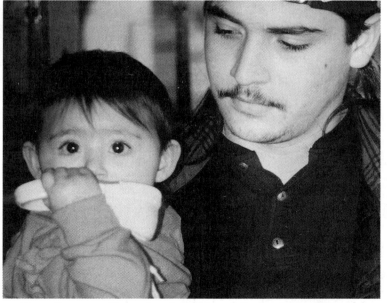

Sometimes you'll need to hold him while you're in the store.

When you're in the supermarket, keep your toddler beside you or in the seat in the cart. If he runs down the aisle, don't expect him to come back when you call. He's not yet ready to follow commands from a distance. Instead, go after him. Take his hand or gently pick him up. Tell him he must sit in the seat in the cart to avoid getting lost or injured.

When he's in the cart, it's easier to talk to him. Discuss the items you're buying and how you plan to use them. Perhaps he could hold the can of tomatoes or help put some carrots in the bag. Your child will have an easier time shopping if he feels that he's helping you shop and not just waiting for you to get the job done. If he's involved, it can be a good learning experience, too.

> *Heather used to get away from me and hide. She thought it was funny. I didn't.*
>
> *After this happened a few times, I talked to her before we went in. I told her if she did that again, she couldn't go with me next time. It worked.*
>
> Eve, 19 - Heather, 2

A few children go through stages of being extremely difficult to handle in a store. If shopping has become a frustrating experience for both you and your child, avoid taking him to the store if you can. If you have no other choice but to take him, try to keep the trips short and infrequent. Try not to go when he's tired.

Discipline in the supermarket may be more difficult than at home. If you can be consistent with him, even in the middle of a crowded supermarket, you have learned a marvelous lesson in practicing good discipline.

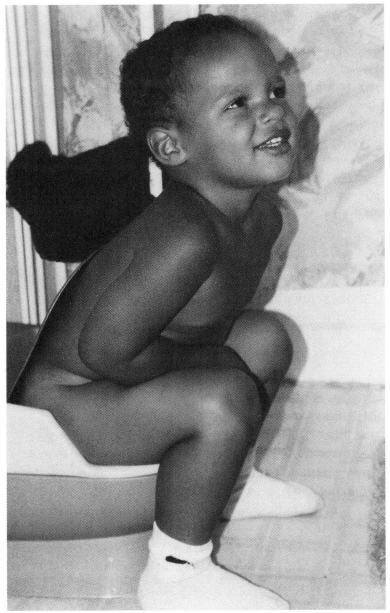

Using the toilet can be exciting and rewarding.

9

Don't Rush
Toilet Teaching

*All my kids have been different
about going to the bathroom.
Steve was past 3. He said, "I
don't want to." Then one day
he decided to use the toilet,
and I haven't had a problem
since.*

*Elaine was 18 months old. I
was working at the time, and
her babysitter was training her
twins who were a year older.
She asked if it was okay to try
Elaine, and it worked.*

*Mike was very reluctant.
He'd pull his underwear off
and get another diaper. I went
back and forth with him. We'd
quit for a month, then try*

again. One day he was ready. I think he was at least 3.
I never pushed my kids to use the toilet. I always
had the feeling that when they were ready, they
would.
                Angelina, 28 - Steve, 13; Elaine, 10; Mike, 8; Patrick, 2

Considering the Word — Training

"Toilet training" is a strange term. We tend to use the
word "training" when we're talking about teaching dogs
and horses. "Teaching" seems more appropriate for
children.

Some people think toilet teaching simply means you
guide the child to sit on the toilet, and you tell him to
perform. Success will naturally follow. Unfortunately, this
is not the case.

First of all, toilet teaching should seldom be considered
for children under two. Most children aren't ready to use
the toilet until after their second birthday. Some are quite a
bit older.

Actually, successful toilet teaching depends much more
on development than guidance. He won't be able to urinate
or defecate reliably in a potty chair or toilet until he can
recognize his need to go and has developed some control
of the muscles that control the release of urine and
BM (feces).

Teaching him to sit on a potty chair before he's ready is
quite meaningless, a waste of time for both of you.

Toilet training Antoine was the hardest thing for
me to do. Just trying to get him to say he had to go to
the bathroom was difficult because he would never
say he had to go potty.
   He was two when we started. He was telling me
"No" about everything. He was talking, so I figured if

*you can talk and say all these other things, then you
can tell me when you want to go potty.*

*I had to take extra clothes everywhere we went,
and it took a whole year. By his third birthday there
was no problem.*

Elysha, 21 - Antoine, 4

Life would have been much easier and less frustrating
for both mother and son if Elysha hadn't bothered with
toilet teaching during that difficult year. If you start toilet
teaching when your child is already saying "No," you
probably won't be successful.

Chances are that Antoine would have been using the
toilet just as effectively on his third birthday if his mother
had waited almost that long even to suggest he do so. He,
like many children, apparently wasn't ready at age two.

Respecting Your Child's Feelings

Attempts at early toilet teaching must seem strange to a
child. Imagine you're a toddler. Your mother puts diapers
on you for months. She changes them when you get them
wet or messy. Then one day she puts another kind of panty
on you, and suddenly it's an "accident" if you get those
panties wet or dirty. Confusing.

You'll save yourself and your child a lot of frustration if
you cheerfully diaper him until he decides he wants to use
the bathroom.

*If you can afford disposable diapers, or have the
use of a washing machine for cloth, what's the big
deal for the mother if the child isn't potty trained? It's
not as if you're standing in front of a washboard
all day.*

*Jarrod was 3 when he was trained, and he has had
perhaps three accidents. The summer he was two he*

would go on his little potty chair by himself as long as he had his diaper off, but not if he had anything on. If he had any clothes on at all, even his training pants, he wouldn't go.

We bought him a small potty. We also got one of those that sets on the toilet, but he never did like that one because it was too wobbly.

Until he was old enough to stand at the toilet and go by himself, he didn't go. But when he did, after about two or three days, he quit wearing diapers altogether. He never even needed them at night.

I have a friend who has made the big girl panties into such a huge reward that to put diapers on her daughter at night is punishment. I don't think that's right. We're talking about physical capacity, a bodily function you can't control for a time.

Jennifer, 23 - Jarrod, 5; Jason, 2; Robin, 11 months

Signs of Readiness

Toilet training Adam was easy. He practically taught himself. He'd follow us to the bathroom, and he liked to sit on the toilet. He'd see us going to the bathroom and he wanted to be like us, but he wasn't quite ready.

I started to get him underwear, and he liked it. Soon he was standing up and peeing nearly every time. When he had an accident, we'd say, "That's okay, that's an accident."

Leona, 18 - Adam, 4; Cami, 1

You may decide it's time to try toilet teaching if your child has a dry diaper for long periods of time. Or perhaps he seems to be interested in the toilet or potty chair and wants to sit on it and use it. Or he may tell you when his diaper is wet and he wants it changed.

Remember, before he's ready to learn to use the toilet, he needs to be able to recognize the feeling caused by a full bladder. He must also be able to release his urine flow or hold it back when he wishes.

Likewise he needs to be able to control his bowel movement. He must be able to realize when it's about to come, and to hold it until he can get to a toilet.

>*Lorenzo was potty trained by the time he was 2. I tried to give him a head start before he was 2 and he didn't like it, so we didn't do it any more.*
>
>*The first time we tried it, he was scared, so we didn't do anything about it for quite awhile. I'd try it once in awhile, but as long as he didn't like it, I wouldn't push at all.*
>
>*When he would pee in his underwear, I wouldn't get mad at him. We'd remind him. He'd usually say "No," but we wouldn't get upset. Sometimes we'd just take him to the bathroom.*
>
>*How could you get mad? They're just barely learning. There's a process they have to go through with everything. You can't expect him just to hop on the toilet right away. Punishment would scare them more.*
>
> Guadalupe, 20 - Lorenzo, 4

Some children get this control around two. Many other children don't have it until they're close to three or even older.

Make It as Easy as Possible

If you think your child is ready, put him in training pants. For some children, getting rid of the bulky diaper and being able to wear special training pants helps them become much more interested in using the toilet.

Next, find a comfortable potty seat and encourage him to use it about once every hour during the day. Set him on it for only a few minutes each time. Stay with him and help him feel comfortable.

If he resists sitting on the seat and can't relax, you can figure he's not ready.

> *She was starting to rip off her diapers after she wet them. I said, "If you're just going to rip them off, you can sit on the potty chair."*
>
> *At first she thought it was a chair to play in. So I said, "You sit on your potty chair and I'll sit on mine." Finally one time she went in there. She was real easy.*
>
> *Since I've started potty training her, she has had only two accidents. At first she just wanted to pee, not have her BM. She'd ask for a diaper, then have a BM in the diaper. Then she'd want to be changed. I'd*

Toilet teaching depends on her readiness.

*dump the BM in the potty chair, and within a week,
she was using the chair itself.*

*Then she started wanting me to go out and close
the door. She's so independent. She wants to do
everything for herself.*

Marijane, 18 - Elena, 23 months

Accidents? Try Again Later

*I potty trained Jeremy when he was almost two. It
took about two months for him to where he would
always tell me he had to go potty. When he knew when
he peed in his diaper, I figured it was time.*

*At first I was getting mad when he had accidents.
"You're supposed to tell me," I'd say.*

*My husband said, "Don't get mad or he really
won't tell you."*

*So then I'd say, "You had an accident? Next time
you can go to the bathroom." He's doing real
well now.*

Ernesta, 20 - Jeremy, 3; Osvaldo, Jr., 5 months

Even when a child seems ready for training, he may have
difficulty holding or releasing his urine at will. If, after a
week or so of teaching, the child is still having many accidents, it's best to delay training for another month or so.

Punishment Doesn't Help

*Francene was having accidents. It was time for her
to be potty trained about the same time Alina was
born. I wanted her off the bottle and out of diapers
before I had the other baby.*

*I tried to reward her. I tried spanking her. I told
her she had to sit in her room. I tried sitting in the
bathroom with her. I tried everything. The doctor said*

this often happens when a new baby comes.
We had to live with it for two years. So we
changed. We quit spanking, and we started to reward
her when she did go. Now she does well, but for two
years it was real hard.

I felt it was time to get her out of diapers, and she
peed fine, but she would hide in a corner and go to
the bathroom in her pants. I'd know what she was
doing, and I would say, "What are you doing,
Francene?" and she would just cry. When things like
that happen, I feel there's a problem somewhere.

Joanne, 23 - Francene, 4½; Alina, 3; Gloria, 1

Don't punish your child for accidents. Toileting can't be forced. A child who feels pressured will be tense and unable to urinate when he chooses. He will be even more likely to have accidents. Joanne was correct about there being a problem somewhere.

First, Francene was only 18 months old when Alina was born, and she probably was not nearly ready to use the bathroom.

Second, as the doctor pointed out, when a new baby is born is usually not the time to expect the older child to get out of diapers. To the older child, it seems the baby gets all the attention. If the baby wears diapers, maybe that's why he gets the attention. Therefore, the older child might reason, wearing diapers is the key to getting attention. He may think that losing attention means he's losing your love.

Third, "living with it" for two years means Francene was scolded for two years for urinating and defecating — normal acts except she did them in the wrong place by her parents' standards. That obviously was a difficult time for Francene and for her parents. Continuing to put diapers on her for another year or even two might have prevented a lot of unhappiness.

When your child has an accident, calmly clean it up and put clean clothes on him. He has not misbehaved; it was an accident, and he should not feel ashamed.

Be Generous with Praise

When he does use the toilet, you want to praise him. Tell him how happy you are that he was able to do that. It helps if other family members let him know they're proud of him, too.

If your child spends much time in a daycare center, or with grandma or another caregiver, it's important that you all work together with him when he's ready to go to the toilet.

Let Him Watch

First I bought the potty chair. Jose already knew more or less what I wanted him to do because he would go into the bathroom with me and his dad all the time. I put his potty chair there, and he'd watch us. We'd also tell him what we wanted him to do.

The first time he peed he got all scared. He stood up and got pee all over. I was all excited and I clapped my hands. Then he wanted to be on the big toilet, so we put the potty chair away.

Now Jose likes to go to the bathroom in new places. We go to the store and he says, "I have to go to the bathroom." We go to someone's house, and "I have to go to the bathroom." He likes his big-boy pants.

AnnaMae, 20 - Jose, 2½

If you can do it without too much embarrassment, the ideal way to teach your child how to use the toilet is through modeling. You show him how. If you encourage your child to sit on his little potty chair while you're on the big toilet, he'll probably get the idea faster.

After all, he wants to mimic you when you're washing dishes and raking the yard. Mimicking you while you're on the toilet may also appeal to him. Most important, instead of putting pressure on your child to use the toilet, you're modeling for him the method you want him to learn.

"Parents Get All Worked Up"

Jim Mead, founder of For Kids Sake, Inc., a parent support group in Lake Elsinore, California, says efforts at toilet teaching result in more child abuse than does any other aspect of childrearing. Parents get all worked up about it.

This is one battle the child always wins. There is no way a parent can make a child urinate in a particular place. This is one area in which the child is in control, an infuriating situation for many parents.

One technique Mead suggests is freezing colored ice cubes. Drop several in the toilet. If your child, boy or girl, urinates on them, the ice will crackle and pop as the warm urine melts it. Fun!

Making urinating fun for the child is more important for the parent than for the child himself, explains Mead. If the parent can join in a little silliness with the child, s/he is less likely to get so angry that s/he hurts him. Mead has seen far too many children physically abused by their parents because they weren't using the bathroom in the way their parents wanted.

Denae's son, Dorian, at 11 months, is not ready to use the toilet. When he is, she says she'll put Cheerios in the toilet and suggest he shoot towards them. Sounds like a good idea.

You Must be "Ready" Too

If you have decided it's time to teach your child to use the bathroom toilet, are you ready? This is an important part of the whole procedure. Do you have time? Can you stay in the bathroom with her? Can you praise her successes? Ignore her failures?

If your parents are having out-of-town company, can you handle puddles on the floor? Sometimes people try to toilet teach their child right before going to see grandma. That's not a very good reason or a very good time.

When you think she's ready and you're ready, put training pants on her for two or three days. She can get them down easier and faster than diapers.

If your child piddles on the floor, don't scold her. Just clean it up. If, after two or three days, she still piddles on the floor regularly, it must not be time for the training pants. Put diapers on her again without showing any disapproval. If she's not ready, she's not ready. That doesn't mean she's bad.

Even after training has been going quite well, some children start having frequent accidents again. If this happens to your child, don't be concerned. Handle the accidents calmly. If they occur too often, diapers may need to be used until the child seems ready to try using the toilet again.

Some children learn to use the toilet quite easily while others have a more difficult time. Because every child is different, there is no one sure method or any particular age that is best for all children. Your child will learn when he's ready.

If you get discouraged, check out the kindergarten class down the street. You'll probably not find a single child in diapers. Your child, too, will learn to use the toilet.

You can help him learn to handle disagreements without fighting.

10

Teaching Your Child
to Avoid Violence

How will I teach Blair to be street-wise? I'd tell him, if you have a problem and you don't know anything about these people, just walk away. Just be a bigger man and walk away from it because you don't know what kind of person this is. He could be real crazy, and that could be the end of you.

I'm more worried for males because they think they have to stand up to people, not look like a sissy or a punk. I'll tell my son it's not worth losing his life, or having a lifetime of problems, or ending up in jail.

Brooke, 18 - Blair, 3 months

Teaching Your Child to Be Non-Violent

There are a lot of gangs at school. I think this means I'll have to be more protective of Casey. I also have to be a friend to him so he'll talk to me. At least I can tell him the way I feel about it. I don't really like gangs. I don't think there's any point in fighting over streets you don't even live on, or over a color.

I don't want Casey to be violent at all. There are other ways to deal with problems. Talk with the person, not fight. Guns turn up here by 6th grade, and it gets real dangerous.

Charity, 17 - Casey, 18 months

You can't immunize your child against being the victim of a drive-by shooting, but you can help her learn ways of avoiding violence. Helping your child learn non-violent techniques for settling disagreements is a gift you can give her that can last a lifetime.

It starts with the relationship you build with your child. The bonding that happens between a mother and her newborn, a father and his newborn, is where it begins. The result of that bonding is healthy attachment between you and your child. This attachment is extremely important for your child's development.

First, when the bonding goes well, you can communicate with each other. Good communication can demonstrate your respect for your child. A child who is respected from birth and whose parents "are crazy about him" is likely to have good self-esteem. You're helping build that self-esteem when you praise him for his accomplishments, when you cheer him on for each step of his development.

What does bonding mean when you have a toddler? An important part of it is the two of you enjoying doing things together. Don't expect him to entertain himself all the time.

Of course he will/should play independently part of the time, but he also needs your full attention frequently.

Language skills are extremely important. If you keep your relationship strong, it should be fairly easy to talk together, and that provides some protection for your child. It helps him learn to use words rather than violence.

Children Learn Violence

No, we don't believe in hitting. All that does is teach the child to hate. When you hit her, you hurt her mentally and physically. You're her parents, and she looks up to you. When you hit her, it really hurts her.

It's better to talk to her, and she won't hate you. She won't grow up in violent ways, thinking hitting is okay.

Nathan, 20 - Dakota, 11 months

A child learns to be violent when her parents are violent. When dad and mom fight, yell, and hit each other, or hit her if she misbehaves, she'll see fighting and hitting as ways to solve problems. It must be all right to hit people. The persons who mean the most to her hit.

I don't spank but I've been tapping his hands if he touches something real bad and he doesn't want to listen. I'm getting to the point where I have to stop, though, because lately if I tap his hand, he hits me back. He's learning how to hit.

Grechelle, 16 - MacKenzie, 11 months

Some parents go beyond modeling violent behavior. They deliberately teach their sons and daughters to be aggressive and to fight. They even threaten to punish their children for *not* fighting. Some parents tell their children to fight back "when necessary." They think that's all right.

A child who sees his parents fighting and yelling will probably fight also. A child who is pushed to be aggressive in his relationships and encouraged to fight will likely tend to be more violent.

If you model nonviolence in your daily life, in your actions with your child as well as with other people, he is likely to follow your example.

To avoid violence, your child also needs to understand how to settle disputes or conflicts without provoking fights or violence. He can begin to learn this skill as he interacts with his family.

If you give your child choices and opportunities to negotiate simple disputes such as food or clothing choices, he is likely to try to follow your example. For instance, sometimes he may offer another child a toy when what he wants is the toy the other child has. Rather than just grabbing the toy away from the other person, he's attempting to negotiate. He may not always be successful in these early attempts but he's beginning to learn the valuable skill of negotiation.

Be Your Child's Advocate

First of all, I don't think you should fight to solve a problem because that makes the problem worse. Glen tells Leonardo, if a kid hits you, go and tell the teacher or tell your mom. We don't tell him to fight back.

Kerrianne, 19 - Sergy, 3; Leonardo, 4

If your child tells you another child is hitting him or threatening him, what should you do? How can you be an advocate for your child? You could go over to the school and talk to the teacher in a non-accusing way.

Discuss what you understand happened from what your child said. Your child should be there with you. If there are any questions, he can answer them. He will see that both you and the teacher are trying to help him.

You might tell the teacher you're trying to raise your child in a nonviolent way, and you're trying to prevent fighting, but your child needs to be protected. Ask the teacher how you can work with her to protect your child. *You have to be an advocate for your child.*

> *Basically I'll teach Clancy what my parents taught me. If somebody hits you, first tell somebody rather than act on impulse and smack him back. If it happens where he's on the street, and somebody starts messing with him, go to a nearby store or knock on some-body's door and get help — at least to call me.*
>
> *I'll try my best to teach him to walk away rather than to fight.*
>
> Chelsea, 19 - Clancy, 2 months

Dealing with Angry Feelings

Even if you've grown up with violence around you, you can learn better techniques for handling problems. It's important that you learn these techniques, not only for yourself, but even more for your child's sake.

You can help your child learn ways of dealing with angry feelings in nonviolent ways.

> *I've seen a counselor for anger management, and it helped 100 percent. They can help you out with your frustrations, with your family, other problems. I can bite my tongue now. If we got in this fight right now, who is going to get in trouble? If you have a back-ground with the law, you get your kid taken away if you fight. It's hard to walk away, but I've learned to do it. Yesterday I walked away from my worst enemy.*
>
> Samantha, 16 - Kaylie, 20 months

There was a time when many people expected their sons to fight. A boy who refused to fight was labeled a sissy. Some people still feel this way.

This kind of thinking was based on the assumption that boys were not likely to be seriously injured in a fist fight. Guns were not supposed to be part of the deal. Now, however, the widespread use of guns drastically changes the situation.

I'll teach my son that if he can walk away from the problem, walk away. But if the problem is going to follow you, you may have to handle it. But you have to think it through. What's going to happen if I beat up this guy and he gets a gun?

Riley, 18 - Dorian, 11 months

Being able to walk away is important, and sometimes it's a really hard thing to do. Your feelings are hurt, you're angry. Some people are too afraid to simply walk away.

Counting to ten before reacting helps some people calm down. Sometimes cracking a joke will cut the tension. Walking away from an argument may be the best approach. Then angry feelings have a chance to cool down. Usually, expressions of anger only create more problems.

Your child watches your response in any dispute. From his observations, he gets ideas on how to respond. He's likely to copy the strategies he thinks work. When you avoid conflict, you're helping your child. From your example, he's learning safer ways to handle situations that could become dangerous.

What I learned from the streets myself, you can either turn the other cheek or you can stand up and fight, but to stand up and fight may not be the right thing to do. I want him to understand there are

consequences to every act he takes. I hope he can
speak his way out of it.

Domingo, 22 - Lorenzo, 4

Encourage your child to talk to you. Really listen to him
as he tries to express his thoughts and feelings. This will
help him gain confidence in his ability to use words.

With your help, his use of language will continue to
grow and improve. He will become more able to talk to
other people and solve problems with words. You are
helping your child learn how to use words instead of fists.

I tell my sister, if somebody hits you, walk away
because all it's going to do is get you in trouble. My
mother told me when I was 5 to hit back, but I tell Sis
to walk away. Sometimes you have to defend yourself,
but usually fighting is not going to solve the problem.
It will just make it worse.

Bridget, 18 - Barnaby, 6 months

Keeping Guns and Children Separate

Most of my friends older than me have guns. All
that's going to do is get them killed or put them in
prison. They'd bring their violence to their house, and
what if his son got hurt? I'm so afraid of guns. I don't
like guns at all. About five months ago I was there
when a real close friend got killed.

Bridget

Guns are one of the leading causes of death in children.
Although many people have guns in their homes, seldom
do they teach children how to handle them safely. Often
they don't even store the guns locked up in a safe place.

When young people handle guns, it can be dangerous not
only to their enemies, but to family members and friends as
well. It can also bring more violence to their home and

family, increasing the chance that someone will be killed.

If you have a gun in your home, be sure it's locked away from your child. Don't put it in a glass case where he can see it. The gun should not be in sight, it should be unloaded, and the ammunition should be stored in a different place. You want to be absolutely sure your child or another child isn't killed by a gun in your home. An alarming number of guns in homes are used against family members.

Some people believe playing with toy guns desensitizes a child to the deadly reality of guns.

> *I don't like my kids to play with guns. I don't think they're old enough now to know the difference between a real gun and a toy gun. I don't let them even have a water gun. I will buy them anything else but not gun toys.*
>
> Kerrianne

Effect of TV Violence on Your Child

> *I think violence on TV can lead to violence. I don't let Leah watch violent movies. If she watched that stuff, she'd probably get scared and have nightmares.*
> Lyra, 18 - Leah, 2½

The television shows your children watch have an impact on their behavior. Researchers have observed children at play before and after watching violence on television. Sure enough, their play becomes more aggressive after watching the violence on the screen. Deborah Prothrow-Stith, M.D., author of *Deadly Consequences* (1991: Harper), writes (page 45), " . . . researchers have learned that the greater the amount of violent television a child watches, the more violent his or her interaction with peers is likely to become, and these effects linger."

Limit the amount of time he spends in front of the TV set. Carefully select the programs he sees. Try to keep him from watching those with a violent content. If your child should watch a show with strong emotional content, and he's old enough to talk about it, ask him how he felt about what he saw. Listen patiently to his reply. Encourage him to continue if he seems to want to talk some more. Discussions like this can make a difference in your child's approach to conflict.

Other Techniques for Dealing with Violence

In addition to giving your child the gift of loving, firm, and *gentle* discipline, you can help him learn the skills that will go a long way in protecting him from violence.

Helping him develop his mind is an important part of protecting him. You will be helping him grow intellectually. He will be able to learn how to handle conflict without resorting to violence. He will be better able to reason and consider other solutions. He will want to try harder because he will have confidence in his ability to succeed.

Where does intellectual development begin? It starts at birth. Talk to him. Describe the things you do for him, the things he sees, the way things feel. Talk to him about everything, and he will listen. This is how he learns about language and how to communicate with people.

Read to him. At first he may mostly enjoy the sound of your voice, but this will change. First, he will enjoy picture books, then simple stories. Eventually he will develop a love for books and reading.

As he grows older, share stories and videos that demonstrate handling disagreements without violence.

Play with him often. Find games and toys to use that are fun for both of you. These will change as he grows older.

All of these kinds of experiences with you and other caring adults are important to a young child. They will help her grow intellectually. They will help her be smarter. She will be ready for school when she's old enough to go.

Children who do well in school are less likely to act on their anger, less likely to be overly aggressive than is the child who does not perform well at school and is not secure in his feelings about himself. Prothrow-Stith states (page 171), "The children who think they're smart go to school and get smarter. The children who think they're dumb go to school and get dumber." An important part of your job is helping your child understand what a good person he is, and helping him develop his talents and abilities.

Again according to Prothrow-Stith, the research shows that children who learn to assert themselves without verbally or physically attacking others are less likely to become bullies. They are also less likely to become victims of bullies.

Richard Tefank, Chief of Police, Buena Park, California, works with many families whose children are deeply involved in gangs. He thinks teens who choose to avoid gang activity usually have strong parental influences at home, and they know that such activity is not acceptable to their families. They are also strong personally to be able to survive that peer pressure. They are street-wise and smart enough to walk that tight rope, and not become a victim of the neighborhood.

For ten years, the Buena Park Police Department has been offering parenting classes to parents of teenagers involved in gangs. "We often hear parents say, 'We don't know how to control our child's behavior,'" Tefank commented.

Parents tend to think it's the material things they give their child that matter. If they can't give the child material things, the child will think they don't love him. Not so, Tefank says emphatically. The love and emotional support you give your child are far more important. It's the child who doesn't get that love and support at home who goes to the gang to get it. Then, if the child becomes a parent, s/he tends to parent the way they were parented. It's a hard cycle to break.

For a more in-depth discussion on parents' involvement in gangs and its impact on their parenting, see *The Challenge of Toddlers* (Lindsay).

Importance of Consistent Discipline

Two important guidelines stressed in the parenting classes offered by the Police Department are the same as those stressed in this book:

1. Don't forbid an activity unless it's harmful to your child or to other people and/or property.

2. When you do give your child direction, see to it that he complies. As we've said so often, that doesn't mean hitting him to "make him behave." That almost never works, except for a short time. It doesn't teach him self-discipline. You want him to behave as he should not only because you say so, but because he learns to control his own actions.

Consistently practicing your loving and firm discipline strategies with your child will help him avoid the violence all around us. *Together, you'll both be winners.*

Parenting is sometimes frustrating, often rewarding.

11

Focus
on Mom and Dad

*It's hard being a mother. I
can't do a lot of things I want
to do because I have to take
care of Mona. To me, it's hard
raising kids. I thought it would
be easy.*

*Sometimes it gets on my
nerves, and I feel like hitting
her. I give her a bottle instead
and tell her to shut up. I can't
stand it when she cries
and cries.*

*Layne and I got married
before Mona was born, and
it's hard. Too many bills, and I
have to get a job because
Layne doesn't make that much.*

Ellie, 17 - Mona, 11 months

Double Challenge for Teen Parents

Whether you're a single parent or you and your partner
are parenting together, you have additional challenges as
very young parents.

Whatever your situation, you're facing the usual challenges of parenthood. In addition, you have the extra challenge of meeting your needs as a teenager. While you probably matured a great deal while you were pregnant, you
still need to enjoy life. (Older parents, of course, have the
same need.) Friends are still important. "Acting like a teenager" occasionally is important to you and your partner.

Difficult as it may be, you have a double task as a
parent. You aren't "just" somebody's mother or father. You
are you, an important person with needs of your own. See
Your Baby's First Year and *The Challenge of Toddlers* for
suggestions on meeting your needs for a satisfying life now
and in your future.

How you feel about yourself and your life plan has a big
impact on how you discipline your child. If your life is not
going well at this time, you're likely to have a harder time
parenting.

As a teenager, you're still maturing at a fast rate. You're
still becoming the person you want to be. You're still
discovering the person you are. You want to try new things
to discover your potential.

Now you must balance your needs and goals with the
enormous responsibility of raising a child. It's not easy.
Some parents set aside too many of their own goals while
others may not meet their parenting responsibilities
adequately.

"She Does What She Wants"

Setting limits and enforcing them takes a lot of time. It's
hard for some teen parents to take time to teach their child

in this way. One young mother who was asked for comments for this book responded:

Jeanne, sorry. I can't help with this topic. I can't help but give my daughter what she wants when she wants it. This has become a habit, and I don't know how to break it without hurting her feelings or her hurting herself physically.

Gloria, 19 - Katy, 2 1/2

The young mother went on to explain that she is extremely busy. She is a college student who is involved in many activities on campus. She's a member of the college pep squad and an officer in several clubs at the college.

These are rewarding activities. Parenting a child is also a rewarding activity, however, and it is a commitment she made when she became a parent. If Gloria no longer has the time or energy to discipline to the best of her ability, she needs to eliminate some of her outside activities. She needs to find more time for Katy. A toddler "who is always given what she wants when she wants it" is not likely to be a happy, or even a safe child.

Angelica explained this concept well. She had a different reason for allowing her toddler to do whatever she wanted:

Shaun was spoiled for several months because I had a problem with drug abuse. I'd let him do whatever he wanted because that was easier. Then my mom helped me, and I went into recovery.

Things are going a lot better now. When I let Shaun have everything he wants, our relationship goes down the tube, and he doesn't like me very much. If I always let him have what he wants, he knows something is wrong. I think that's the biggest reason I've been able to stay clean. I didn't like us not liking each other.

Angelica, 20 - Shaun, 3

Raising children is one of the most important and most stressful things that people do. It takes an enormous amount of love, patience and plain stamina to accomplish the task.

Frequently young parents don't get the support they need. Finding enough money for adequate housing, food, and clothing may be difficult. Finding time for relaxation and friends or even enough rest may seem impossible.

Parenting Is Stressful

This is not what I wanted — going to school when I have a baby. I wanted to be the at-home mom. I think when babies are raised where the mom is there all the time, they're more secure.

It takes putting your life on hold for awhile, like going out. A lot of us didn't have good nurturing parents, and it's hard to be nurturing when you weren't given the nurturing.

Zandra, 16 - Dakota, 11 months

Young parents living on their own may feel themselves under a great deal of pressure. Besides the financial problems, there is stress involved in starting a new family along with school and/or a new career.

It may be a big benefit to the children if the mother can stay home during the early years. For many teen mothers, however, this is not possible. Even if it is, it's not likely to be easy for her. Having several small children makes it doubly difficult to meet all their needs, let alone mother's and dad's:

Francene says, "Come on, Mommy, let's draw together," and I say, "Not now." I always put it off. She's asking for that time with me but Gloria always crawls over to us, and Alina wants to do whatever

we're doing. I'd like it to be just me and Francene,
but I can't.

When Alina comes in crying —sometimes I get real
frustrated about my own life and I take it out on my
kids. They say, "Why are you mad at me, Mommy?"
and I will say, "I'm sorry. I'm having a bad day."

You know, I have no time for myself at all. I take
care of them, I take care of my husband, and I have no
time for myself.

Joanne, 23 - Francene, 4 1/2; Alina, 3; Gloria, 1

Finding occasional release from childrearing pressure is
important even if it just means going to the park with
another parent and having an opportunity to talk while you
watch the children play. You and your child may feel more
relaxed when you get home. Joanne continued:

I notice that the more we do with our kids, the more
they don't fight, the more loving they are. I notice
when I push them away Francene tends to break her
toys or yell back. When I take my time to sit and listen
to her tell me what she did at school, the more
attention I pay, the better she is.

Julio spends time with his friends, and he says, "I
work all day and I deserve this." I feel that way, too,
but we can't do that because we have three kids. We
need to spend more time with them, more picnics on
the weekend.

We had a nice weekend this week. We bowled on
Friday night, and the kids were in the babysitting
place at the bowling alley. We went over to my mom's
afterward.

Francene spent the night over there and Alina
wasn't upset. When Francene came home the next
day, we rented a movie and had ice cream.

Your Self-Confidence Is Important

To discipline a child well, you need to have confidence in your ability to parent. Remember the parenting skills you've been learning and use them to build a trusting relationship between you and your child. This relationship is what makes discipline work.

This relationship is very important to your child. She needs to know that you believe she is a good person who is capable of learning and achieving new goals. She also needs to know it is safe to make mistakes along the way.

A parent who honestly believes her child is deliberately naughty needs to look at what has gone wrong with this relationship of trust and try to fix it.

Spanking doesn't work. Forcing your child to submit to your wishes through fear of punishment will only lead to a need for more punishment and a lot less trust.

Alina is 3, and in my opinion, she knows right from wrong. When she hit the "No" stage, if I didn't spank

Two or more toddlers complicate parents' lives.

her when she needed it, she would run all over me.
They have to know I'm the boss. They know if they do
bad, they will be punished. I spank them if they don't
listen.

Julio, 23 - Francene, 41/2; Alina, 3; Gloria, 1

Julio and Joanne have three children under five. Finding
time for a positive approach with each toddler is difficult.
But does spanking really help? In chapter 6, we point out
that spanking doesn't seem to accomplish much over time.
In fact, Julio adds:

It's a touchy subject. Some people don't hit their
kids, and they come out perfect. I was abused, and I
came out okay. A buddy of mine can beat his child
and he'll go right back out there and do it. It makes
you wonder.

There was a time when people believed that spanking
worked. These days most people know better. In fact, now
in some countries, it is illegal to spank one's child.

A power struggle with a toddler helps neither parent nor
child. Set the limits you need and maintain them consistently. Let your child be in charge when possible. Trust her.
Give her a chance to learn self-discipline.

If Mom and Dad Live Together

Kendall and I would fight and we'd yell. Kaylie
was always there, seeing us arguing, and it wasn't
healthy for her. She started getting violent, she started
getting rough. She doesn't talk, but she would scream
and point her finger at us.

I told Kendall, "You know, we have to argue some-
place else because look what it's doing to Kaylie."

When we finally broke off our relationship, she was

crying, screaming, hitting dolls, throwing fits. We
were together for a year, and it's been two months
since we broke up. Kaylie still fights a lot, and I tell
her it's no good — but she will still laugh. She thinks
it's funny.

Samantha, 16 - Kaylie, 20 months

A child who lives with fighting and violence will feel
this is normal behavior. Of course she will imitate it in her
play and in her life. This is how she has observed the
significant people in her life behaving.

If you live with your partner, your relationship with each
other has a big impact on your child. Joanne observed:

I know that when my husband and I fight or argue,
it really bothers the kids a lot. When you're angry or
upset you don't stop to think it's hurting the kids.

The other day we decided that whenever we get
upset at each other, if the kids are around, we'll just
talk about it instead of yelling. If we can't do that,
then one of us will take a walk or go to the bathroom.
We'll wait until the kids aren't around to fight. They
love their mommy and daddy, and when we're
fighting, it upsets them a lot.

My parents argued a lot, and it upset me. Both
Julio and I are from broken homes, and I have always
said that no matter what is wrong, we brought three
kids into the world and they love us both.

If we separated it would really hurt them. I know it
damaged me and my three brothers when our
parents split.

Joanne

Parental anger is very difficult for children to handle.
The angry voices and the strong feelings expressed are

frightening. Some children feel that they're somehow responsible for the outrage expressed.

Parents need to spend time together with the children, but also alone with each other. Their relationship needs to continue to grow and develop. Then when differences arise, they will be easier to handle.

Building a strong relationship takes commitment and hard work, but it's worth the trouble. Parents need to find ways to discuss their differences and work out solutions to their problems. It's not always easy. If they're unable to work it out, they should seek help and guidance.

Sharing Childrearing Beliefs

Me and my boyfriend have different standards for discipline. He lets Bronwyn go further than I do.

We talk about it but we haven't resolved it. I won't spank. My dad spanked me a lot, and if somebody raised their hand at me, I cowered away. I don't want Bronwyn to go through that.

Hillary, 17 - Bronwyn, 10 months

You and your partner need to share with each other your ideas on childrearing, especially in regard to discipline. Most parents have strong feelings about how a child should be handled. If one parent has been brought up by parents who spanked a lot and the other wasn't, it may be hard for them to agree on discipline methods for their child.

Some parents are very anxious about the things a small child might do or the problems he could cause. They fear the worst. They tend to be overly restrictive in their childrearing practices. If you or your partner feels this way, you need to discuss both your reasons and your feelings in an effort to agree on discipline strategies. Most feelings about discipline are the result of what the parent experienced as a young child.

You and your partner need to be together on discipline. Never argue about what happened in front of the child. Your child has to see that you both stand behind the same rules and consequences. Otherwise, if you're fighting back and forth, he'll play you against each other.

Diane, 19 - Lee, 3; Zach, 1

There should be as little conflict as possible between parents. When parents disagree on methods of discipline, the child will soon learn to play one parent against the other, as Diane said. He may manipulate them to get what he wants. This is certainly not a goal of good discipline, and it is damaging to family relationships.

Yoko and her husband are finally able to talk through most of their disagreements on discipline issues:

Most of the time Nelson and I agree. When we don't, we have a pow-wow in our bedroom where there are no kids. We discuss our points and try to work out a compromise. Sometimes one of us comes around to the other's point of view, and we agree that way. We know the most important thing is that the child always know he's loved, no matter what.

Yoko, 25 - Sheila, 9; Matthew, 6; Karena, 2

Father-Child Time

When my husband comes home from work, he tries to have his time with the kids. He takes the dog and goes for a walk with them. And if he's able to pick Francene up at school, she just glows. Being with their dad means a lot. He's like Francene's role model and Alina's prince. Daddy is their everything.

Joanne

Dad is often tired when he comes home from work. He may have little energy left for playing with active little children. However, most children look forward to a special playtime with their dad. When this happens, a bond develops between father and child that brings pleasure to both.

I feel a father should be involved. Your child is only young once. Once they grow up you can never ever get that back. You should spend as much time with them as you possibly can. By doing that, you see your child progressing, and you don't miss out on her life.

I feel my family is more important than anything else in my life. My job can come and go, but every year my child gets older, and I will never get that back.

Me and Elena, we have our time together. I try to spend as much time with her as possible. Sometimes when I'm working, I'm exhausted when I get home. She will run around and say "Daddy, daddy," and I'll sit there comatose. But I like to play with her and she likes it, too, or I read her a story. She loves books.

Raul, 19 - Elena, 23 months

In many homes, mom is the only parent. In other families, dad is present but mom does most of the parenting. If dad is involved in caring for, playing with, and disciplining his child, he probably considers himself a big winner. Being an involved and loving parent is truly a rewarding experience.

If Dad Is Gone for Awhile

Often it's hard for young parents who live together to agree on discipline techniques. If they aren't together for a time, the absent parent may have a tough time catching up on the needs of his/her child(ren).

Dawn Ellen's boyfriend joined the Army two weeks before she realized she was pregnant. After much long-distance discussion, the young couple decided to marry. Their wedding was four months before Mercedes was born. Frank wasn't able to come home for nearly a year after the wedding. Dawn Ellen remembers:

Her father first met Mercedes when she was seven months old. He was here about a month, and we had trouble because he has different ways. We didn't bring her up together.

Frank was back again at Christmas when she was 18 months old. It was a little easier this time because she pretty much could do for herself, and we weren't arguing quite so much. When he's here, she loves her daddy, and she's always with him.

We haven't seen him for more than a year now.

Dawn Ellen, 19 - Mercedes, 3

Other parents are gone for months, even years, because they're in jail. Keeping in touch with their child and the child's other parent during this time takes lots of effort and determination from both parents. If a parenting class is available, participating in it might help the absent parent understand better the stages through which their child is going. They'll have an idea of the behavior they can expect when they return home.

If one parent is away temporarily, the parent at home needs to try hard to keep the absent parent informed of their child's development. Letters, photographs, and phone calls become extremely important.

Sometimes Separation Is Best

The first 2 1/2 years we lived together, but he was gone a lot. When he wasn't around, Destiny was very good. When he'd come around, she stopped talking, she stopped potty training, and she was on the bottle until she was two.

Finally I said it was the drugs or us. He'd leave for three months and tell me he was clean. Then I'd find he was into it, and he would leave again. I don't know why I stayed with him so long.

Madge, 18 - Destiny, 3

It's a pity that so many young people are lost to drugs. This child needs a father on whom she can rely. Madge needs a partner who cares. A parent on drugs is not likely to be responsible.

Parenting — You Can Do It!

Raising your child is a difficult, time consuming, challenging job for which you may have had little training. At times you may feel frustrated. You may be bothered about the times you didn't discipline well.

Use your discipline techniques on yourself:

- Don't be too hard on yourself when you make a mistake. You'll get another chance. Next time you can do it better.

- Don't give up. Think of other ways to help her learn. Try again.

- Be patient with your progress. Learning a new skill takes time and a lot of effort.

- Praise yourself when you succeed. *You deserve it!*

Sometimes a teen parent feels she's missed out.

12

When Too Much Goes Wrong

Inside I'm screaming. I just want to run away from everything, from all my problems, but I can't do that because of Clancy. He has nothing to do with my problems. I have to learn how to cope with the stress.

I think some teen parents take their frustration out on their kids, and I don't think that's right. I try the best I can to keep my cool for Clancy's sake because I don't want to do to him what my parents did.

When I was growing up and my parents got frustrated, they'd take it out on me. They

*abused me. My mom would pull my hair, and one time
she kicked me down the stairs. That's what I don't
want to do with Clancy. I want to be able to sit back
and take a couple of breathers. I want to be able to
say, "Clancy, I can't handle this now. Mommy has to
sit back and take a breather."*

*I keep it all bottled up inside me. When I can't take
it any more I either cry or I get real ticked off and I
won't talk to anybody. Nobody has ever told me how
to handle stress. I like to write, so sometimes I write
in a journal when I'm upset. Usually this helps.*

Chelsea, 19 - Clancy, 2 months

Some Parents Feel Trapped

Many teenage parents must feel they've missed an
important part of their growing-up years. Sometimes they
feel trapped. Perhaps they feel pushed into parenthood
before they're ready. It's hard to raise a child. It's even
harder if you're still very young yourself.

A mother may feel shut up with her child day after day,
isolated from her friends and lacking both time and money
to do the things she enjoys. Newly married or out on her
own, she may miss the companionship and support of
her parents.

Parents need support. Mom needs a friend she can trust,
one who will listen to her complaints and frustrations. She
needs someone she can lean on who will help her when she
needs relief from the stress of rearing a child and learning
how to manage a household. She needs someone she can
depend on who cares about her.

Dad, too, needs support. He may be overwhelmed with
the responsibilities he has undertaken. If he can't find a job,
or if the job he has doesn't pay enough to support his
family, his frustration may be enormous.

At the same time, he probably has little time or energy left to relax with his friends or to spend on activities he used to enjoy. Instead, he'll come home to a tired partner who needs his support and a baby that needs and wants his attention. There may be little if any time left for the parents to enjoy each other's company.

"I Gave Up All My Childhood"

It's nearly impossible to raise a child with patience and understanding if you don't have the support you need for yourself. Colleen is in that unhappy position:

I gave up all my childhood to marry Charles and have a baby. Being grown-up is a lot of responsibility. Like now, it seems all I have is responsibility. I don't have any fun. My soap opera and smoking are the only entertainment I have. I used to drink but I gave it up completely.

If I had known what I know now, I probably would have had an abortion with Hilda. If I could advise anyone, I would tell them to wait until they have done what they wanted to do. I feel like I'm sacrificing for the kids. It seems like I don't ever have the joy of it, I just have the cleaning. Charles has the joy because he comes home from work and plays with them, but I don't have any real joy.

Sometimes I go in the bathroom and shut the door. When Charles comes home, he asks what I'm doing shut up in a little box, and I tell him that's my privacy. I would rather have them older.

Colleen, 18 - Ruby, 7 months; Hilda, 21 months

A young mother may feel cheated. She may have dreamed of having a baby she could cuddle and love. She expected a baby who would nurse with little effort, smile at her a lot, and sleep through the night within a few weeks. Somehow, this rarely happens with real babies.

Childrearing is stressful and sometimes thankless. The baby demands and needs attention day and night. The mother may have been unprepared for the tiredness and loneliness she is feeling. She feels others criticize her.

Dad may feel left out. He may feel mother has time only for the baby.

Parents need to feel good about themselves. They need and deserve recognition and praise for the demanding job they're doing. Childrearing is a difficult task. It demands lots of maturity.

A teenager's goals and value system aren't going to change overnight to those of an adult just because she's now a mother. If she's home all day and doesn't have time to be a teenager, frustration may build up. She needs to do something about it before she becomes overwhelmed with the stress and takes her anger out on her child.

Considering Options

Most parents resent their children at some point. If they understand that these feelings are normal, and they don't react by hurting their child, they'll be able to get past a temporary crisis without too much trauma. If, however, the resentment happens often, problems with discipline can too easily result in child abuse.

Occasionally a mother will realize this is not the right time in her life to raise a baby. With too few resources and too little support, she is unable to provide for her child's needs in a way she feels is right.

Because she loves her child and wants him to have a better start in life than she can provide at this time, she may consider an adoption plan. It's a difficult decision to make, but making an adoption plan for her baby may be the most loving thing she can do if she finds she's unable to cope.

Sometimes a mother keeps her child for poor reasons. She may regard caring for her child as a sort of penance for an indiscretion. She was probably told to avoid sexual intercourse. Now she must pay the price. For her, her baby is a constant reminder of her error.

Both she and her baby deserve better. Raising a child should not be considered a punishment. There are many couples who desperately want a child to raise, but are unable to have one of their own. They have a lot of love to give, and are at a point in their lives when they have the time and money to handle the responsibilities of parenting.

An adoption plan should never be made before examining all possible options. This includes finding information about available support resources in the community. No one else can make an adoption decision for the mother and father.

Teresa's Story

Teresa found an opportunity to examine her options. Her son was born when she was 16. Teresa lived with her mother, but her mother was gone most of the time.

One night when Eddie was about two months old, he cried steadily from 11 p.m. to 2 a.m. Teresa tried to feed him, tried to comfort him. Nothing seemed to work. Finally he went to sleep, and she got a few hours rest before school started. That morning Teresa wrote a note to her teacher describing her feelings:

Please help me. I felt like hitting Eddie last night. I'm scared. What can I do?

At her teacher's urging, Teresa shared her feelings with the infant center director. She also made an appointment with a social worker from Children's Home Society.

As she talked with Pat, the social worker, Teresa realized she needed some time to consider her feelings, to think through her situation. She agreed to put Eddie in foster care for a short time. Two weeks later she called Pat. "I'm ready to bring Eddie home," she said.

Life didn't suddenly become easy for Teresa. But with continuing support from the infant center staff and occasional talks with Pat, she was able to care for Eddie and continue school. She graduated when he was fourteen months old.

Three years later when Teresa, now married and living in another state, heard that her teacher was working on a book for teenage parents, she wrote:

> *I think you should include something about child abuse and neglect. People feel as though it will never happen to them. But you and I know that no matter how good a parent you are, it can still happen. It can be dealt with if you look for help and can confide in someone as I did.*
>
> *I think that subject is too often avoided, as if it doesn't happen. People have to realize it does exist. They need to know where they can turn for help.*
>
> Teresa, 20 - Eddie, 4

Consequences of Too Much Stress

A young mother, home all day alone with her child in a small apartment, often finds it difficult to cope with just one toddler. If there are two or more small children, it can get pretty miserable for everyone.

Colleen, quoted earlier, had too much to do caring for Ruby, seven months old, and Hilda, 21 months. Too typical of her own and her children's lives was the following incident:

Hilda was holding a paper cup with a lid. She had a drinking straw she was trying to put through the tiny hole in the lid. It wouldn't go in. She kept poking the straw at the top of the cup, getting more and more upset. Soon she was crying in frustration.

Hilda's mother's reaction was, "Shut your mouth right now." She spanked Hilda, then took her to the bedroom as she screamed, "Wait right there until you calm down." She slapped her, then yelled, "I mean it, Hilda, sit there until you calm down." Then she slapped her again.

Hilda came out of the bedroom and tried again to put the straw in the cup lid. She started sobbing again because it wouldn't work. Mother screamed, "Knock it off, Hilda, or you go back in the bedroom."

This anecdote may seem almost unreal. If mother had paused just long enough to show Hilda how to stick the straw in that hole, this crisis might never have occurred.

Put yourself in that young mother's place. She has another smaller child. She doesn't like her husband much. Money never lasts until payday. She hates her apartment. Yet she knows no way out.

These are the kinds of conditions that produce a climate for abuse. Once abuse begins, it's hard to stop. Trust in the child is replaced with poor expectations. Guidance is replaced by force. The parent vents his/her rage, and discharges his/her frustrations. The abuse escalates.

Children raised by angry hostile parents are likely to be angry aggressive children who frequently get into fights and other serious trouble. They may always have difficulty getting along with people. Many jail inmates suffered from child abuse.

Child abuse occurs more often with children under three

than any other age group. The abuse can easily lead to
tragedy if it is not stopped.

Children Can Be Exasperating

All of us have times when we feel physically ill, have
problems at school or work, or problems getting along with
other family members. There are times when things seem to
be going wrong far faster than we can handle. That's when
a child's demands may seem too much to endure.

All of us get up-tight with our children. All of us at some
point have trouble controlling feelings which could lead to
abuse. When one feels isolated or depressed, it's easy to
blame the child for everything that's going wrong.

> *Sometimes if you're just staying at home, you've
> had it, and you shouldn't feel bad. You feel like you're
> going crazy and no one else is like this. When I feel
> like this, I try — it doesn't always work — to sit down
> and read for awhile. I always try to relax when the
> baby is asleep, at least an hour when I do nothing
> except watch TV or read.*
>
> *Sometimes I just have to pull myself together and
> calm down. It isn't easy. You have to remember you
> aren't really bad for sometimes not liking your kids.*
>
> Celia, 20 - Laurel, 4; Lance, 18 months

It's even harder for a parent who was abused as a child
to deal with childrearing stress without resorting to an
abusive response. She's likely to repeat the harsh measures
she endured herself — even though she probably promised
herself she'd never do it.

What Is Child Abuse?

There are several kinds of child abuse. Probably the one
most often mentioned is physical abuse. The child may be

struck, shaken, or otherwise attacked. He is deliberately hurt. Cuts, welts, bruises, burns, or even broken bones or other internal injuries may result.

Such injuries may be the result of punishment. The physical injury can also result in psychological trauma. The child often doesn't even understand why he was hurt.

Neglect is another form of abuse. A child may be left unattended or isolated with no one to answer his cries. He may be confined and lack opportunities to learn. He may not have enough clothing, or he may be dirty and smelly from lack of washing or diaper changing.

He could be undernourished or improperly fed, not given the food necessary for growth and development. The food may be unclean or improperly cooked. He may not have a decent place to sleep, eat or play. Any of these conditions may indicate neglect. Neglect also occurs when the child's medical needs are unmet.

Sometimes parents feel isolated and lonely.

Some children have to endure psychological abuse. They are yelled at, threatened, and put down in frightening ways. The psychological injuries that result leave no visible marks, but can be a serious problem for the child for the rest of his life. He will become anxious and fearful. Anxiety can interfere with many aspects of normal life.

Even sexual abuse can occur in the preschool years. See *The Challenge of Toddlers* for suggestions for protecting your child from this kind of abuse.

A child who is unfairly treated by his parent(s), the authority figure(s) in his life, may have a difficult time trusting and reacting appropriately to other authority figures such as teachers, his bosses, police officers, and others.

Value of Support Group

If you feel isolated and lonely and are often depressed, or if you frequently have angry irritable feelings and find little joy in caring for your child, it's time to do something about it. There are parent support groups in most communities. These programs often have activities or childcare for children along with information on childrearing. The parent has a chance to be with other parents who are experiencing similar problems. S/he won't feel so alone.

Learn about the resources in your area. Check with your local school district. There may be a teen parent program or an adult school program that can help. A community service center listed in your phone book under city government may suggest a program. There are often programs in parks.

If you're receiving TANF (Temporary Aid to Needy Families), your social worker may have some suggestions. Your priest, pastor or rabbi may offer some help, too.

Childrearing information is important. Understanding child development will make your parenting job much easier. You won't waste your time trying to make your child do things he isn't ready to do.

Development can't be forced. You'll learn to cope with your toddler's self-directed and self-centered behavior when you realize they relate to his emotional and intellectual development.

As you begin to understand the learning process, you'll be more in tune with your child's joy of discovery. You'll begin to enjoy him, have fun with him. You'll be rewarded with some of the pleasures of parenting.

Who Needs Help?

How does a parent decide if s/he needs further help? We know that all of us feel very angry at our children occasionally. It's how we react to those feelings that is important.

Jim Mead, Director, For Kids Sake, Inc., a parent support group in Lake Elsinore, California, offers a "National Parenting Test."

National Parenting Test

1. Do you sometimes strike your child without thinking?
2. Do you feel better after you spank your child?
3. Do you sometimes spank your child with a belt or switch?
4. Are you the only one who takes care of your child?
5. Do you sometimes leave bruises or marks on your child when he's bad?
6. Does potty training upset you?
7. Does your husband or wife sometimes hurt the children and you're afraid to say anything?
8. Do you sometimes feel sexually attracted to your child?
9. Do you feel relieved when you yell at your child?

10. Does your child's crying and screaming make you mad?
11. When your child is bad, does it remind you of your childhood?
12. Is your child different from other children?
13. Do you punish your child for toilet accidents?
14. Do you sometimes leave your child alone when you know you shouldn't?
15. If you could give your child away without any questions asked, would you?
16. When you were a child, were you ever abused physically or mentally?
17. Do you use drugs or alcohol to feel better?

Mead asks parents to take this test, then add up the number of "Yes" answers they have. He thinks most parents will answer "Yes" to at least one question. These parents are probably "normal" loving parents who lose their cool occasionally.

Mead thinks those who answer "Yes" to four or five questions may have a high level of frustration or hostility. He urges these parents to get professional help.

If six or more questions are answered "Yes," Mead recommends professional counseling for the parents. He also strongly suggests the children be given a vacation with grandma or another loving relative or friend while their parents receive counseling. These aren't necessarily bad parents, but their frustration level has gotten so bad that it has gone beyond their coping skills. They need help.

Assistance for Abusive Parents

Help is available almost anywhere in the United States for parents who are abusing their children or think they might be close to doing so. One of the best resources is

Parents Anonymous (PA). It was started more than thirty years ago by a mother who was involved in child abuse. With some help from a professional counselor, she and other parents who were abusing their children started meeting together to talk and offer support to each other.

More than 800 chapters of Parents Anonymous are now in operation in the United States and Canada. You can contact any of these groups at any time of day or night. Either find their listing in your local telephone directory or call their national office, 909/621-6184. You can follow the phone prompts to get a resource in your area.

Members of PA meet in small groups with a professional sponsor. They share the confusion and anger with which they struggle. They support and encourage each other in finding positive ways to cope with the job of childrearing.

Apparently PA works. Independent evaluators have found that physical abuse usually stops within the first month of the parent's involvement in the organization.

Your county or state Mental Health Association can probably refer you to a number of local counseling programs. Get their phone number from the information operator or your phone book.

Your local college or university may be able to direct you toward help. Call their psychology department and ask about local counseling programs.

After sharing the above suggestions, Mead added, "If you have tried all of the above ideas and aren't satisfied, call For Kids Sake, Inc., 909/244-9001, 24 hours a day. We will try to assist you in finding help in your area."

If you need to find help, do it now before the situation becomes worse. Abusive parenting produces physical and emotional scars that can endure throughout the child's lifetime. The welts and the bruises may fade away, but the psychological damage remains to haunt him.

He loves time with Grandpa.

13

When Grandparents Help Discipline

- **Sharing the Discipline Responsibility**
- **Grandparents Feel Quite Involved**
- **May Not See You as Primary Caregiver**
- **Different Rules Confuse Your Child**
- **Sharing an Already Busy Household**
- **Meals with Toddlers**
- **What You Can Do**
- **Effect of Taking Responsibility**

It's hard living at home. They spoil Janet. I didn't want that to happen, but it's happening. My mom lets her get into everything. During the day I tell her, "No." Then when I come home after my mom has taken care of her, she's spoiled rotten.

Candi, 16 - Janet, 18 months

A lot of us live here —me, my two boys, my grandpa, my mom, my sister, and her two girls all live here. If I could live just with my kids, I think I could discipline them so much better.

My mom always spoils

*Ricardo — she thinks he can do no wrong. She gives
in to him, and it's hard to do anything with him. I
guess I spoil Raul. Everyone says I do.*

Evangelina, 18 - Ricardo, 3½; Raul, 27 months

Sharing the Discipline Responsibility

Living with both parents and grandparents can be bliss
for a toddler if it means more people to love and care about
her. It can help her feel confident and secure, and provide a
wonderful environment for growth and learning.

If you live with your family or your partner's family, it
also means there will be more people dealing with your
child's behavior. You need to share your ideas on child
rearing and come to some agreement with your family on
how to discipline your child. Ask them to read some of the
books or pamphlets that you've found helpful. Perhaps
you'll want to share this book with them.

Other family members are more likely to support your
discipline ideas if you take most of the responsibility for
childcare. However, if grandma babysits a lot and grandpa
provides financial support, they will feel they have a right
to be involved in rearing your child.

*Ryan and I lived with my parents the first three
years. My parents were getting after me for getting
after him so much, yet they were annoyed at the things
he did — so I'd get after him more.*

*Even now, when I visit them, my parents will tell
Ryan "Yes" after I've said "No." I'm finally to the
stage where I can look them in the eye and say, "I
said 'No' for this reason." Now we can go home if my
dad says, "This is my house and he'll do what I say."
When I lived there, there wasn't much I could do.*

Kristin, 23 - Ryan, 8; Tiana, 4

Your parents feel they already understand how a child should be disciplined. Even if they don't consider themselves experts, they know they've had more experience than you have. After all, they've already raised a family.

They may feel that allowing your child more freedom means more problems for them. They may feel comfortable only when your toddler is confined to a relatively small play area or a playpen. They probably remember accidents that happened to you. They're concerned that your child will hurt himself during his reckless explorations.

They may worry about the mischief he will get into and the mess they may have to clean up. They may worry about things he will break or carry off and lose. Thorough child-proofing may be impossible with older children at home.

You may feel your child is being needlessly restricted. When you try to explain this to your parents, you may appear to get nowhere.

If you don't want to resort to hitting as a method of disciplining your child, you may get a lot of complaints from your extended family:

> *It's changing now that Shelly is older and has her own personality. When she does something wrong, my mother and sisters hit her hand. Or when she does something, they'll tell me, "Hit her," and I'll say, "Why?" I don't think that's right when she didn't know what she was doing wrong.*
>
> *If she does something wrong, I want to tell her what it is. I don't want to hit her hand like they tell me to. They think I'm being too soft, and that she'll walk all over me later on.*
>
> Dixie, 18 - Shelly, 17 months

On the other hand, you may feel your parents are too lenient. They give him anything he wants, and they don't support your efforts in setting limits and maintaining those limits.

> *When Leesha was born we lived at my mom's. Leesha had all kinds of people disciplining her, and she was spoiled. If someone yelled at her, she'd run to someone else. With Manuel, we're on our own and we do what we think best. It's working a lot better.*
>
> Kambria, 19 - Leesha, 5; Manuel, 14 months

They May Not See You as Primary Caregiver

> *It's hard for me to discipline Victor because I live with my parents and everything I do is wrong. If it was my choice, I wouldn't be here, but I have no place else to go. I can't even tell Victor "No" because they'll go behind my back and give in to him.*
>
> *To tell you the truth, I've never disciplined Victor except maybe at school. My dad thinks of him as his, not even as my son. I wish I could sit down and tell my parents how I feel. I know they love Victor, but I'm the one who should discipline him.*
>
> *Actually, he don't feel like my son. Just because I had him doesn't make him feel like he's mine. Like if he's wearing something they don't like, they'll change him. If I feed him, they'll take it away and feed him something else. It's a problem.*
>
> Raylene, 18 - Victor, 2

It's often hard for the grandparents to recognize the mother as the primary caregiver of her child if she's living in their home. You probably are still dependent on your parents for many things, and they may see both you and your child as their responsibility.

When other family members discipline, too, you need to agree on what your child is allowed to do. It will cause a lot of confusion if grandma slaps her hand for touching the china vase, eight-year-old Aunt Susan hits her for grabbing her doll, and fourteen-year-old Uncle Joe laughs at whatever she's doing.

Different Rules Confuse Your Child

> *Vanessa is real spoiled, and it's hard to discipline her. When we're alone, she listens to me, but when other people are around, she goes crazy. I live here with her father and my mother-in-law. Vanessa doesn't listen to my mother-in-law because she spoils her. She lets Vanessa have her way all the time.*
>
> Rene, 18 - Vanessa, 19 months; Shavone, 1 month

It's hard for your child to accept or even recognize limits when each caregiver imposes different rules. When expectations for behavior vary widely, she must test limits frequently. She will seem to be undisciplined and spoiled.

Some grandparents feel they have a right to spoil their grandchild a little, and that it's the parent's job to discipline him. They may think that giving in to the child's wishes is a way to ensure the child's love. They may not even be aware of the confusion they're creating in the child's mind when they contradict the parent.

If family members don't come to an agreement on how discipline is to be handled, the child learns to be manipulative. He tends to go to the person who is most likely to give him the answer he wants. Should he not like it, he'll try someone else. Some people find this behavior in toddlers amusing, but it won't be very funny when he's older.

Sharing an Already Busy Household

Some young parents and their child need to live in already crowded households until they can afford to get out on their own.

Sometimes a young child has trouble adapting to a home bustling with activity. There may be little space for toys and play. Activities begun may be interrupted or spoiled. It's frustrating for her, and makes it hard for her to learn.

If she can't concentrate on the things that interest her, your child will be restless. She may get into a lot of mischief. She may seem spoiled and undisciplined. Interrupted eating and sleeping schedules make matters even worse.

Another child living in the family home can add to the problems. The other child may resent having the toddler in the home. If there is little living space, the toddler is more likely to get into his things and break them.

Discuss these problems with other family members. Perhaps you can find solutions. There may be no easy answers, but through cooperation, can you arrange some play space especially for your toddler? This could help you all work out an agreement on discipline strategies. With his own play space, he's less likely to bother the older child.

Meals with Toddlers

Problem

Ricardo and Raul aren't very good eaters. They're always up and running around. I fix them lunch, but I don't sit there and make them eat. Usually they eat about an hour before dinner, and then at dinner they'll eat a little. Then they're off running around.

My mom says they should sit there and eat. She says I'm starving my kids, but I feel they'll eat what they want. It's not like we all eat at the same time or sit at the same table and eat together. Some people sit at this table, and some at another. We don't sit down together for dinner.

Evangelina

What do they eat an hour before dinner? If you give them another snack, they won't be hungry at dinner time. If you don't give them something, they'll be fussy and irritable. The best solution may be to serve part of their dinner now. A few vegetables served raw or quickly cooked in the microwave could hold off hunger for a little while.

While it's nice if everyone can sit down to eat together and enjoy a time of companionship, it simply isn't possible in many families. If you and your family don't sit down together at dinner, you might like to try having part of your dinner with your children. Most toddlers will eat better with some companionship.

A toddler is often a fussy eater with a very poor appetite. He needs some structure at mealtime to help him concentrate on the job of eating. Try to give him his dinner at about the same time every day. Find a comfortable place for him to eat that is suited to his small size. Hopefully, if you are there with him at mealtime, talking to him and encouraging him, he will enjoy his meal a little more and will eat a bit better.

Grandparents and other family members may have definite opinions about how and when a toddler should be fed. The child's messy eating habits, the small quantity of food he eats and the large amount of food that appears to be wasted may create problems in the family. Many grandparents have lived through hard times, some on a very tight budget. The wasted food may seem quite intolerable.

Others may sincerely feel the child is being malnourished and should be forced to eat more food. The parents and the grandparents need to listen to each other.

If nutrition is a concern, write down everything the toddler is eating for a week. The record may show that he is getting enough food. It's also possible the record will suggest some changes in his diet.

What You Can Do

Trying to rear your toddler in your parents' home may
be difficult, but you don't need to give up your childrearing responsibilities. There are things you can do.

First of all, try to limit your complaints. You may not
always appreciate what other family members are doing,
but if it really doesn't matter, forget it. However, if you feel
something is wrong, ask them to stop. Tell them what you
want done instead. For instance, "My doctor feels Joey
should not eat cookies. I bought some crackers. He can
have crackers for a snack instead."

Use a positive approach. Tell your parents how you want
your child to be treated. Praise them when you like what
they do. Thank them for their extra help. Parents are far
more likely to cooperate and to provide the help you want
and need if they feel their help is appreciated.

Discuss your ideas on childrearing with them often.
Listen to their viewpoints, too. Show them magazine
articles or books on discipline that you think are good.

Work with them to reach some agreement on discipline.
This is so much better for your child than listening to
constant bickering among the significant people in his life.

Effect of Taking Responsibility

If your parents know you're eager to take the responsibility for rearing your child yourself, and you're doing the
best you can to cope with it, they're far more likely to go
along with your wishes on discipline.

*Sometimes my folks tell us what to do with Dustin.
Most of the time we agree between us what we want to
do. If it's something different from what my mom and
dad or her mom and dad want, we go to them and say,
"We know you take care of him, you discipline him,*

but we want this done when he does this," and they say, "Okay."

Like with bottles. When we took him off the bottle, that was it. We threw them away. Then my dad got him a bottle. We said, "No more bottles."

My dad said, "That's my grandchild, and I'll get him a bottle if I want to."

We said, "This is our child. Do you want to watch him the way we want, or do you want us to take him somewhere else?" Ever since then he has respected our wishes.

We almost always come to an agreement. Once we all agree that it will benefit Dustin, then it's okay. Sometimes it's they who explain to us the reasons they want something done differently, and sometimes we agree.

Mark, 22 - Dustin, 2½

Mark and his family live by themselves. When the parents don't live in the grandparent's home, problems caused by differences in childrearing philosophy are usually easier to work out. There is less pressure on the relationship.

If parents and grandparents can openly share their opinions on childrearing in a non-critical way, everyone benefits. Although extended family relationships can be exasperating, they are valuable and well worth working out.

Grandparents often provide valuable support for teenage parents and their children. With this support, the young family will be more able to grow toward the independent living they probably would prefer.

If you're in this situation, grandparents and other extended family can provide a sense of added security to you and your child. Your child knows many people love and care for him. *He is a lucky child indeed.*

She's a busy, curious child who wants to please you.

14

Ten Strategies That Work

- **Use "No" Sparingly**
- **Self-Control Develops**
- **Use Positive Approach**
- **Distract Her**
- **Communication and Respect**
- **Offer Consistent, Balanced Lifestyle**
- **Give Him a Choice**
- **Reinforce Behaviors You Like**
- **Warn Her Before Activity Change**
- **Time Out May Help**
- **Provide a Reward**
- **Strategies Instead of Punishment**

Right now I just pick up Robin and move her if she gets into something I don't want her to have. I put her in another corner of the house, or I take the item away and put it up high.

Melinda, 15 - Robin, 9 months

She's thrown only a couple of tantrums so far. We give her a lot of praise when she's a good girl. That's a lot of the time, and we try to reinforce that.

We're fairly consistent. She wants to be a good girl. I think a lot of it is attention. When you give them a lot of attention, they don't have to misbehave.

John, 21 - Mandi, 22 months

Strategies, Not Punishment

In this book we've focused on strategies which will help you help your child behave in a positive way. We've stressed that discipline strategies, not punishment, will be most effective.

These strategies will help you achieve your goal of helping your child grow to be a caring, loving, self-disciplined human being. Many of them have been discussed before. We have selected ten of the most important of those strategies to emphasize in this chapter. We are listing them as tools to help you with a difficult job:

1. Use "No" sparingly.
2. Use a postive approach.
3. Distract her.
4. Provide communication and respect.
5. Offer a consistent and balanced lifestyle.
6. Give him a choice.
7. Reinforce behaviors you like.
8. Warn her before an activity change.
9. Time out may help.
10. Provide a reward.

Strategy 1: Use "No" Sparingly

"No" is an important word in discipline. It's such a valuable word that it must not be spent too freely. Your goal when you say "No" is to get your child to react, to stop what she's doing. If she hears "No" every two minutes all day long, she's not going to respond.

If she hears "No" only a few times a day, and she hears a different I-mean-it tone of voice, she will learn to react and obey. That's what you want.

Test yourself. For one day make a note of every time you say "No" to your child. Also jot down the reasons you said it.

At the end of the day, look at your record. Did you say "No" a lot of times? Each time did you see to it that your child stopped what he was doing?

Were there situations for which you said "No" today, but yesterday you thought weren't important? Perhaps the behavior even seemed funny the last time. Your record may show some interesting results.

When you say "No," you're setting a limit that must be maintained. Before you do this, think about your reasons: Is the object breakable? Does it belong to someone else? Is the activity unsafe? Don't say it if you don't need to.

Perhaps you said "No" because someone else thought you should. That "No" may be much harder to maintain because you may not believe in what you're saying.

You must be consistent. Once a behavior is a "No," it is important that it always remain "No." Otherwise, you're encouraging him to test every "No" he hears. If a forbidden activity is running into the street, you'll have no trouble in being consistent. You'll always react in the same way.

On the other hand, if you don't think the forbidden activity is important enough to make you follow through, don't say "No" in the first place.

She'll ask me if she can have some juice or a popsicle. I'll tell her "No" because it's right before dinner. She'll go to the refrigerator and pour herself some juice anyway and say, "I want it, I get it."

It's real hard. Sometimes we'll take it away from her and say "No, you can't have it." Other times when you look at her face when she says it, there's nothing you can do but laugh.

Cathi, 18 - Susie, 34 months

Laughing at an activity today, then forbidding the same activity tomorrow is confusing to the child. If Cathi doesn't want Susie to have juice, she needs to stop her from getting it. If she decides juice is not a problem, she should be consistent in allowing Susie to get juice when she wants it.

Use "No" only when it's likely to be effective. If your toddler is across the room and deeply involved in an activity, he'll probably not respond to a simple "No." Simply removing him will be much more effective than shouting "No."

Self-Control Is Still Developing

If Marty is doing something I don't want him to do and I say, "No," he'll look at me with his hand moving toward the object I told him not to touch.

He'll look at me as if he's daring me . . . as if he's saying, "Yeah, Mom, you're going to tell me what to do?"

Yumiko, 16 - Marty, 21 months

Sometimes a crawling baby or even a young toddler will go to a forbidden object saying "No, no, no" as she continues on her way. She may even check to make sure her mother is watching.

She may remember she's not supposed to touch it. At this young age, however, she can't always control the urge to do something she wants to do.

Research shows that the baby with a lot of freedom to investigate her house can control her own behavior better than can the baby whose parent constantly tells her what to do and who stops her exploring. A baby who is told "No" a lot actually gets into more trouble than a baby whose caregivers child-proof the house so she can explore with less restriction.

Strategy 2: Use a Positive Approach

You already know that if you use "No" less often you get better results. This doesn't mean you let him do whatever he wants to do the rest of the time.

How do you encourage your toddler to do what you want her to do? Your first problem may be getting her attention:

> *It really bothers me when she says "No" and won't do what I tell her to do — especially when I know she knows exactly what I want. She won't look at me — she just sits there and won't do what I say.*

> John

You need to get her attention first. Stoop down and make eye contact before you tell her what you want her to do. Then she will be more likely to listen to you and to understand what you're saying. Remember, she's getting a lot of information through your body language, too.

When you talk to her, give her positive rather than negative commands. Tell her what she should do rather than what she should not. Instead of saying, "Don't touch the vase," try "The vase needs to stay on the table." Instead of "Stop pulling the cat's tail," try "Let's pet the kitty gently."

You will also find that "You need to . . ." and "You may not . . ." are two phrases that often work well with children. They give clear directions in a non-threatening way.

When you patiently help her understand how you expect her to behave, you're helping her learn your expectations for her behavior. This is an important part of discipline.

Toddlers often resist following directions when they're tired. They're very active, and they tire quickly. Simple fatigue is at the root of many discipline problems. Recognizing this and adjusting your expectations may make life easier for everyone.

Strategy 3: Distract Her

I keep on getting up and taking things away from Casey. I try to occupy him with something else, walk around with him or take him outside.

I don't think spanking and hand slapping is right. They're just curious, and they don't really know what they can get into and what they can't. They're just trying to explore everything.

We don't have a playpen. I think he learns more when he's able to explore.

Charity, 17 - Casey, 18 months

When you distract her from an unwanted activity by giving her something else to play with, you can often do so without using the word "No" at all.

"Here's your ball. Can you roll it to me?" works much better than saying to a nine-month-old baby, "No, don't do that." By offering her alternatives, you're telling her what to do.

Moving her away from the things she can't have, and moving her near toys she can have is much more effective than telling her "No."

Strategy 4: Communication and Respect

Develop a relationship based on communication and respect. Be a friend to your child as well as a parent. Try to make the daily routines fun for him.

At mealtime, tell him about the food he's eating. Discuss the color and the texture as well as how it tastes.

Talk to him as you change his diaper. Tell him what you're doing and discuss how he feels.

You're telling him that all these things you do for him are more than just a duty you must perform. They are something you do because you truly care about him and how he feels.

Play games with your baby. While he's little, they may be simple things like peek-a-boo. Later he'll appreciate your help as he learns to stack blocks and put very simple puzzles or formboards together.

Playing with simple puppets is fun for young children, too. It can be a great communication aid as well. Many children enjoy talking to puppets.

Discipline throughout childhood will be easier if you and your child can communicate easily. *The time to start is now.*

Communication and respect are important discipline strategies.

Strategy 5: Consistent and Balanced Lifestyle

Try to maintain a basic schedule. Young children need some consistency and balance in their lives. Generally they will eat better and get to sleep more easily if these events occur at about the same time every day. If your toddler is well-nourished and rested, he'll be a lot easier to manage.

It is also a good idea to balance active play with quiet play. Too much active play may tire or over-excite him. His behavior may become silly and a bit destructive. But sitting too long is hard, too. His muscles need to move and he must explore. He will cope better with a balance of activities.

Strategy 6: Give Him a Choice

Give him a choice whenever you can. "It's time for your bath. Do you want it in the tub or in the shower?" may get his cooperation faster than ordering, "Take your bath now." "Do you want lunch outside or in your high chair?" may make him more willing to leave his morning play than a command, "Come to lunch right now."

When you give him a choice, you're giving him a sense of control over his environment and a feeling of competence. This means he's less likely to defy you.

Keep the choices simple. Even then, he may have a difficult time sticking to his choice. For instance, if you ask him if he'd like apple juice or milk for his snack time, he may select the milk. Then he may become very upset if he can't have juice instead. Let him change his mind. That's all right.

Be sure the choices you give him are real. Don't ask him "Do you want to go to bed now?" if you've already decided he must go. Point to the clock and say "It's time to go to bed now. Which bedtime story would you like me to read?"

Strategy 7: Reinforce Behaviors You Like

Reinforcing good behavior is an important part of discipline. If, when your child is playing quietly, you ignore him, his behavior is not being reinforced. Instead, join him in his play or talk about what he's doing. For instance, tell him, "I like the way you stacked those blocks." Or sit quietly and watch him play.

Toddlers need a lot of attention. Positive attention from significant persons makes learning more meaningful and important. Praise works so much better than punishment.

If he's getting your attention and companionship when he's behaving the way you want him to behave, he'll probably continue doing those things that draw the attention he craves. If he seems to get attention mostly through being naughty, he'll probably act naughty more often.

Strategy 8: Warn Her Before Activity Change

Many young children have a hard time changing activities. They become quite involved with what they're doing, and it's hard for them to stop. Try to tell her a few minutes ahead of time when you want her to change her activity. Then she knows her play is about to be interrupted, and she can begin to think about what will happen next.

This will help her learn to anticipate and plan ahead. It will make her feel she has control and will make the transition from one activity to the next much easier for both of you.

Your baby will feel better, too, if you offer her the same consideration. When she is on the floor, get down where you have eye contact with her. Then say a few words to her before you pick her up and carry her off. It must be quite startling and a bit scary, too, to be suddenly picked up and carried off without a word of warning.

Strategy 9: Time Out May Help

"Time out," time spent away from stress or over-stimulation, is a respite. It's a time to get one's self back together to deal with the problems that must be faced in life. This is a healthy idea for any person.

A young baby will essentially ask for time out by fussing or crying to be picked up when his immediate environment has become too stressful. Over-excitement or over-stimulation is hard for the young child. A mother may sense this need. As she picks up her baby, she may instinctively turn as if to shield him from the source of stimulation.

Time out can work for a toddler, too. What is exciting fun for one toddler may be stressful or over-stimulating for another. Temperament plays a significant role. Too little activity can be stressful also. If a toddler is required to wait, he will seek activity, and he may become very hard to handle.

The toddler may express his distress by fussing or crying, or he may "act out" and misbehave. Hitting, biting, throwing toys or other objects may be an indication that the child has lost control of his behavior and may need help to regain it.

Time out need not be spent without any activity. It is not necessary or even desirable to set the child on a chair in the corner. It can be time spent resting, or with a quiet activity away from noise and excitement or other stimulation. *The goal is not to punish the child, but to help and support him so he can get back in control.*

Perhaps as he gets older, he will recognize his own need for rest and relaxation. This is more likely to happen if time out has been a positive experience for him, and it has not been used to punish or embarrass him.

Strategy 10: Provide a Reward

A reward for a particular behavior should occur as a natural result of that behavior. For instance, tell him if he helps you pick up the toys, you'll have time to read him a story.

> *If I don't approach her in a positive way — we used to go around and around to do her hair. I would practically have to arm wrestle her — but if I say, "Here is a new barrette," or "Your dad is coming home and you want to look pretty for him," she'll sit on my lap quietly while I do it. She likes compliments just like anybody does.*
>
> Jodie, 19 - Bedelia, 26 months

Finding ways to help your child want to cooperate is much more logical than setting out to prove who is in charge. Everyone enjoys receiving compliments. What a logical way to gain your toddler's cooperation!

Many times the best reward is telling him that he did a good job and that you're proud of him. This is much more significant than saying he's a good boy. By recognizing his ability to do the task and to do it well, you help him feel competent. He'll feel able to learn even more.

Problem

If we're in the mall, she always wants to go into Burger King. She loves Burger King, and if we don't walk in there, she'll sit on the floor in the middle of the mall and scream. It frustrates me.

Sometimes if I have the money we'll go in because half the time we're there, we're going to eat anyway. Other times I make her get up and she'll just have to cry. I'll tell her to stop crying. It's very embarrassing.

LaToya, 20 - LaShan, 3

If a trip to Burger King is on the agenda anyway, perhaps the idea of a contract might make the shopping trip
more pleasant for everyone. Contracts for unpleasant things
are okay. It shows you understand how your child feels, but
that you need his cooperation anyway. A treat at the end of
a long shopping trip when he's already tired helps him feel
a bit more in control, less like baggage.

When a child is at least 21/2, a contract may work. The
idea is to help the child understand that if he will cooperate
and help you, you'll do something he will enjoy. This idea
works better with older children. Very young children have
a hard time waiting for a reward.

Strategies Instead of Punishment

You may be able to think of many other strategies that
will work with your child. Using discipline strategies to
help him behave appropriately will make childrearing much
more effective than using punishment to force him to
follow your wishes. With your discipline strategies, you not
only help him learn self-control, you support his self-
confidence. You give him self-respect.

Discipline is not easy. It is an extremely important and
often difficult part of childrearing. It takes an unbelievable
amount of common sense, patience and practice. It also
takes a deep desire on your part to help your child learn
self-discipline as a first step toward becoming a
responsible, independent adult.

Discipline begins with your relationship with your child.
You have been developing this relationship since she was
born. If you have a good relationship, she wants to please
you just as you want to please her. You want to do things to
make her feel good. She wants to do things to make you
feel good. *Above all, good discipline demands an unending
supply of love.*

Appendix

About the Authors

Sally McCullough worked for thirteen years in the Tracy Infant Center, 11 years as head teacher. This is a model center in the ABC Unified School District, Cerritos, California. She also directed the Tracy Infant and Toddler Program for Children with

Special Needs and Their Families during those years.

Before that, Sally was chairperson of the Nursery School Board, then Director of the Encino Presbyterian Nursery School in Encino, California.

Sally completed a Bachelor's degree in psychology. She and Stuart have three grown children and four grandchildren.

Jeanne Warren Lindsay is the author of fifteen other books dealing with adolescent pregnancy and parenting. She, too, has worked with hundreds of pregnant and parenting teenagers. She developed the Teen Parent Program at Tracy High School, Cerritos, California, and coordinated/taught in the program for sixteen years. She continued as a consultant for several more years. Cur-

rently, she maintains her ties with teens through the interviews she conducts for her books.

She has completed graduate degrees in Anthropology and Family and Consumer Science. She and Bob have five grown children and five grandchildren.

Bibliography

The following bibliography contains books of interest to pregnant and parenting teens. Workbooks and other classroom aids are available for some of these titles. The address and phone number of a publisher is listed only with the first resource described.

Prices quoted are from *Books in Print,* 1997-1998. Because prices change so rapidly, however, and because publishers move, call your local library reference department for an updated price and address before ordering a book. If you can't find a book in your bookstore, you can usually get it directly from the publisher. Enclose $3 for shipping per book. See page 207 for an order form for Morning Glory Press publications.

Bjorklund, David F., and Barbara R. Bjorklund. *Parents Book of Discipline.* 1990. 272 pp. $5.95. Ballantine Books.
Emphasizes that discipline is not the same as punishment, but is one of the fundamental ways that parents teach their children to respect others and themselves.

Briggs, Dorothy C. *Your Child's Self-Esteem*. 1975. 360 pp. Doubleday.
This is a classic. Through the use of countless anecdotes about children, the author discusses the value of self-esteem in a human being's life and the important part parents play in the formation of self-esteem in their children.

Crary, Elizabeth. *365 Wacky, Wonderful Ways to Get Your Children to Do What You Want*. 1995. 102 pp. $9.95. Parenting Press, Inc., P.O. Box 75267, Seattle, WA 98125.
Includes hundreds of positive (and sometimes zany) ideas for solving common problems with young children.

_____. *Love and Limits*. 1994. 48 pp. $6.95. Parenting Press, Inc.
Offers parents lots of useful ideas to help their children behave well.

_____. *Without Spanking or Spoiling: A Practical Approach to Toddler and Preschool Guidance*. 1993. 126 pp. $12.95. Parenting Press, Inc.
Book offers dozens of examples and exercises to guide parents in finding the best methods to suit their family's needs.

Eley, Eleanor. **"You and Your Baby: Playing and Learning Together." "You and Your Baby: A Special Relationship."** 1994. 35 pp. each. $2.65 each. Bulk discounts. The Corner Health Center, 47 North Huron Street, Ypsilanti, MI 48197. 313/484-3700.
Gorgeous photos of teen parents and their children on every other page. Each booklet contains helpful information at a very easy reading level.

Green, Christopher. *Toddler Taming*. 1999. $6.99. Random House.
An excellent book written with humor. Good down to earth information for parents of toddlers. Very readable.

Kotulak, Ronald. *Inside the Brain: Revolutionary Discoveries of How the Mind Works*. 1997. 221 pp. $12.95. Andrews McMeel Publishing, 4520 Main Street, Kansas City, MO 64111.
An in-depth look at the latest scientific findings about the brain — about how nature builds the brain then develops it during early life.

Lansky, Vicki. *Games Babies Play from Birth to Twelve Months*. 1993. 112 pp. $8.95. The Book Peddlers, 15245 Minnetonka Boulevard, Deephaven, MN 55345-1510. 1-800/255-3379.
Collection of activities — 20-30 ideas for each quarter of the first year. Assign several activities each week to students for interacting with their babies as part of your ages and stages curriculum.

_____. *Getting Your Child to Sleep . . . and Back to Sleep.* 1991.
132 pp. $6.95. The Book Peddlers.
Book offers a wealth of suggestions for dealing with babies and small
children who don't sleep as regularly as their parents would like.

Leach, Penelope. *Your Baby and Child from Birth to Age Five.*
Revised, 1997. 560 pp. $20. Alfred A. Knopf, 400 Hahn Road,
Westminster, MD 21157. 1-800/733-3000.
An absolutely beautiful book packed with information, many color photos
and lovely drawings. Comprehensive, authoritative, and outstandingly
sensitive guide to child care and development.

Lewis, Barbara S. *A Good Beginning: Enjoying Your Baby's First Year.*
1990. 32 pp. $8.98. New Readers Press, Publishing Division of
Laubach Literacy International, P.O. Box 888, Syracuse, NY 13210-
0888. 1-800/448-8878.
To be hung up like a calendar, it suggests activities for parent and baby for
each month of the first year. Available in English and Spanish.

Lighter, Dawn. *Gentle Discipline: 50 Effective Techniques for*
Teaching Your Children Good Behavior. 1995. 107 pp. $6.
Meadowbrook Press, 18318 Minnetonka Boulevard, Deephaven,
MN 55391.
Author believes teaching children good behavior is much easier, more
productive, and more pleasant than focusing on punishing bad behavior.

Lindsay, Jeanne Warren. *The Challenge of Toddlers. Your Baby's First*
Year. 1998. 224 pp. each. Paper, $12.95 each; hardcover, $18.95
each. Workbooks, $2.50 each. **Board games: "Baby's First Year"**
and **"Challenge of Toddlers,"** developed by Diane Smallwood,
$29.95. Morning Glory Press, 6595 San Haroldo Way, Buena Park,
CA 90620. 1-888/612-8254.
How-to-parent books especially for teenage parents. Lots more quotes from
teenage parents who share their experiences with their children.

_____. *Pregnant? Adoption Is an Option.* 1996. 224 pp. Paper,
$11.95; hardcover, $17.95. Teacher's Guide, Study Guide, $2.50/set.
Morning Glory Press.
Birthparents share stories of responsible, difficult adoption planning. Does
*not "push" adoption, but suggests **planning** and deliberate decision-making.*
Stresses open adoption, birthparents' role in choosing adoptive parents.

————. *School-Age Parents: The Challenge of Three-Generation*
Living. 1990. 224 pp. Paper, $10.95; hardcover, $15.95. Teacher's

Guide/Study Guide, $2.50 set. Morning Glory Press.
*A much needed book for dealing with the frustrations, problems, and
pleasures of three-generation living. Useful for helping teen parents
communicate with their parents.*

_____. *Teen Dads: Rights, Responsibilities and Joys.* 1993. 192 pp.
Paper, $9.95; hardcover, $15.95. Teacher's Guide and Workbook,
$2.50 each. Morning Glory Press.
*A how-to-parent book especially for teenage fathers. Offers help in
parenting from conception to age 3 of the child. Many quotes from and
photos of teen fathers.*

_____. *Teenage Couples — Caring, Commitment and Change:
How to Build a Relationship that Lasts. Teenage Couples —
Coping with Reality: Dealing with Money, In-laws, Babies and
Other Details of Daily Life.* 1995. 208, 192 pp. Paper, $9.95 ea.;
hardcover, $15.95 ea. Workbooks and curriculum guide available.
Morning Glory Press.
*Series covers such important topics as communication, handling arguments,
keeping romance alive, sex in a relationship, jealousy, alcohol and drug
addiction, partner abuse, and divorce, as well as the practical details of
living. Lots of quotes from teenage couples.*

Marecek, Mary. *Breaking Free from Partner Abuse.* 1993. 96 pp.
$8.95. Quantity discount. Morning Glory Press.
*Lovely edition illustrated by Jami Moffett. Underlying message is that the
reader does not deserve to be hit. Simply written. Can help a young woman
escape an abusive relationship.*

McCoy, Kathy, and Charles Wibbelsman, M.D. *The New Teenage Body
Book Guide.* 1992. 288 pp. $15. Berkley Publishing, P.O. Box 506,
East Rutherford, NJ 07073. 800/631-8571.
*Crammed with information for teenagers about everything from their bod-
ies, changing feelings, teenage beauty, and special medical needs of young
adults to sexuality, venereal disease, birth control, pregnancy and
parenthood. Lots of quotes from young people, sometimes in the form of
questions.*

MELD Parenting Materials. Nueva Familia: Six books in Spanish and
English. *Baby Is Here. Feeding Your Child, 5 months-2 years.
Healthy Child, Sick Child. Safe Child and Emergencies. Baby
Grows. Baby Plays.* 1992. $10 each. MELD, Suite 507, 123 North
Third Street, Minneapolis, MN 55401. 612/332-7563.
Very easy to read books full of information. Designed especially for Mexican

and Mexican American families, but excellent for anyone with limited reading skills. Ask MELD for catalog of materials for school-age parents.

MELD collaboration. *The Safe, Self-Confident Child.* 1997. $8.95. MELD.
Important information on how to protect children from harm, and ways to help children improve their self-confidence.

Parent Express Series: *Parent Express: For You and Your Infant. Spanish edition: Noticlas Para Los Padres. Parent Express: For You and Your Toddler.* Each newsletter, 8 pp. $4 each set. ANR Publications, University of California, 6701 San Pablo Avenue, Oakland, CA 94608-1239. 510/642-2431.
Wonderful series of newsletters for parents. The first set, available in English and Spanish, starts two months before delivery and continues monthly through the first year of the child's life. Second set with twelve letters covers second and third years. Good resource for teen parents. Beautiful photos, easy reading.

Pollock, Sudie. *Will the Dollars Stretch? Teen Parents Living on Their Own.* 1996. 96 pp. $6.95. Teacher's Guide, $2.50. Morning Glory.
Four short stories about teen parents moving out on their own. As students read the stories, they will get the feel of poverty as experienced by many teen parents —as they write checks and balance the checkbooks of the young parents involved.

Prothrow-Stith, M.D., Deborah with Michaele Weissman. *Deadly Consequences: How Violence Is Destroying Our Teenage Population and a Plan to Begin Solving the Problem.* 1991. 270 pp. $13. HarperCollins.
Book provides a way to comprehend the epidemic of violence that is decimating a generation of young men, especially young black men living in poverty, and offers strategies to stem its tide.

Silberg, Jackie. *Games to Play with Babies* and *Games to Play with Toddlers.* 1993. 286 pp. $14.95. Gryphon House, Inc., P.O. Box 207, Beltsville, MD 20704-0207. 800/638-0928.
Silberg divides games for the first two years into three-month segments and also into categories such as Growing and Learning Games, Kitchen Games, and Special Bonding Games.

Stewart, Nancy. *Your Baby from Birth to 18 Months: The Complete Illustrated Guide.* 1997. 192 pp. $15.95. Fisher Books, 4239 W. Ina Road, Suite 101, Tucson, AZ 84741. 520/744-6110.
Provides clear and valid information about caring for the new baby on up to age 18 months. Well illustrated.

Williams, Kelly. *Single Mamahood: Advice and Wisdom for the African American Single Mother.* 1998. 190 pp. $12. Carol Publishing Group, 120 Enterprise Avenue, Secaucus, NJ 07094.
Down-to-earth, sister-to-sister guide. Offers suggestions on how to deal with work, school, child support, discipline, dating again, and more.

Wonderley, Stan. *Learning Activities for Infants and Toddlers.* 1998. 248 pp. $22.95. Blue Bird Publishing, 2266 S. Dobson, #275, Mesa, AZ 85202. 602/831-6063.
Simple activities using material commonly found in the home. Can help infants and toddlers develop a wide range of skills.

Index

MORNING GLORY PRESS

6595 San Haroldo Way, Buena Park, CA 90620

714/828-1998; 888/612-8254 — FAX 714/828-2049; 888/327-4362

ORDER FORM — Page 1

Please send me the following:

		Price	Total
Books, Babies and School-Age Parents			
—	Paper 1-885356-22-6	14.95	_____
—	Hardcover 1-885356-21-8	21.95	_____
Organizing TAPP: Useful Forms for Teen Parent			
—	*Programs* Paper 1-885356-23-4	4.95	_____
***Teens Parenting* Series:**			
Your Pregnancy and Newborn Journey			
—	Paper 1-885356-30-7	12.95	_____
—	Hardcover 1-885356-29-3	18.95	_____
—	Workbook 1-885356-31-5	2.50	_____
—	**Board Game** 1-885356-19-6	29.95	_____
Your Pregnancy and Newborn Journey —			
Easier Reading Edition (GL3) (1991 edition)			
—	Paper 0-930934-61-x	9.95	_____
—	Hardcover 0-930934-62-8	15.95	_____
—	Workbook 0-930934-63-6	2.50	_____
—	Teacher's Guide 0-930934-68-9	2.50	_____
Adolescentes como padres (1991 edition)			
—	Paper 0-930934-69-5	9.95	_____
—	Workbook 0-930934-71-7	2.50	_____
—	Teacher's Guide 0-930934-72-5	2.50	_____
Your Baby's First Year			
—	Paper 1-885356-33-1	12.95	_____
—	Hardcover 1-885356-32-3	18.95	_____
—	Workbook 1-885356-34-x	2.50	_____
—	**Video** 51 min. 1-885356-02-1	195.00	_____
—	**Board Game** 1-885356-20-x	29.95	_____
The Challenge of Toddlers			
—	Paper 1-885356-39-0	12.95	_____
—	Hardcover 1-885356-38-2	18.95	_____
—	Workbook 1-885356-40-4	2.50	_____
Discipline from Birth to Three			
—	Paper 1-885356-36-6	12.95	_____
—	Hardcover 1-885356-35-8	18.95	_____
—	Workbook 1-885356-37-4	2.50	_____
—	**Video** 52 min. 0-930934-97-0	195.00	_____
Teen Dads: Rights, Responsibilities and Joys			
—	Paper 0-930934-78-4	9.95	_____
—	Hardcover 0-930934-77-6	15.95	_____
—	Workbook 0-930934-79-2	2.50	_____
—	Teacher's Guide 0-930934-80-6	2.50	_____
***Teens Parenting* Sample Kit** — 5 books (4 *Teens*			
	Parenting titles plus *Teen Dads*),		
	5 workbooks, 3 guides,		
—	2 videos, 2 games	498.00	_____

Quanity Discounts Available on Single, Multiple Titles

Total (Transfer to back page) _____

			Price	Total

Novels by Marilyn Reynolds:

		Price	Total
___ *Baby Help*	1-885356-27-7	8.95	_____
___ *But What About Me?*	1-885356-10-2	8.95	_____
___ *Too Soon for Jeff*	0-930934-91-1	8.95	_____
___ *Detour for Emmy*	0-930934-76-8	8.95	_____
___ *Telling*	1-885356-03-x	8.95	_____
___ *Beyond Dreams*	1-885356-00-5	8.95	_____

(Hardcover novels, $15.95 each.)

Breaking Free from Partner Abuse

		Price	Total
___	Paper 0-930934-74-1	8.95	_____
___ *Did My First Mother Love Me?*	Paper 0-930934-84-9	5.95	_____
	Hardcover 0-930934-85-7	12.95	_____
___ *Do I Have a Daddy?*	Paper 0-930934-44-x	5.95	_____
	Hardcover 0-930934-45-8	12.95	_____
___ *¿Yo tengo papá?*	Paper 0-930934-82-2	5.95	_____
	Hardcover 0-930934-83-0	12.95	_____

Parents, Pregnant Teens, Adoption Option

		Price	Total
___	Paper 0-930934-28-8	8.95	_____

Pregnant? Adoption Is an Option.

		Price	Total
___	Paper 1-885356-08-0	11.95	_____
___ *Surviving Teen Pregnancy*	Paper 1-885356-06-4	11.95	_____

School-Age Parents: Three-Generation Living

		Price	Total
___	Paper 0-930934-36-9	10.95	_____

Teen Moms: The Pain and the Promise

		Price	Total
___	Paper, 1885356-25-0	14.95	_____
___	Hardcover 1-885356-24-2	21.95	_____

Teenage Couples: Expectations and Reality

		Price	Total
___	Paper 0-930934-98-9	14.95	_____
___	Hardcover 0-930934-99-7	21.95	_____
___ *Caring, Commitment and Change*			
	Paper 0-930934-93-8	9.95	_____
___	Hardcover 0-930934-92-x	15.95	_____
___ *Coping with Reality*			
	Paper 0-930934-86-5	9.95	_____
___	Hardcover 0-930934-87-3	15.95	_____
___ *Will the Dollars Stretch?*	Paper 1-885356-12-9	6.95	_____
___	Teacher's Guide 1-885356-15-3	2.50	_____

TOTAL (Inc. first page) _____

Please add postage: 10% of total—Min., $3.50;
15%, Outside U.S. _____

California residents add 7.75% sales tax _____

TOTAL _____

Ask about quantity discounts, Teacher, Student Guides.

Prepayment requested. School/library purchase orders accepted.

If not satisfied, return in 15 days for refund.

NAME _____ PHONE_____

ADDRESS _____